BEYOND FEAR

Other books by
ROBERT HANDLY WITH PAULINE NEFF
Anxiety and Panic Attacks: *Their Cause and Cure*

BEYOND FEAR

ROBERT HANDLY
PAULINE NEFF

RAWSON ASSOCIATES

NEW YORK

This book is not intended as a substitute for the medical advice of physicians. The reader should regularly consult a physician in matters relating to his or her health and particularly in respect of any symptoms that may require diagnosis or attention by a health professional.

The names, circumstances and other identifying characteristics of individuals in case histories have been changed to protect their privacy.

LIBRARY OF CONGRESS CATALOGING-IN-PUBLICATION DATA

Handly, Robert.
  Beyond fear.

  Includes index.
  1. Phobias. 2. Fear. 3. Panic attacks.
4. Anxiety. I. Neff, Pauline, 1928–   . II. Title.
RC535.H35 1987 616.85′22   86-42959
ISBN 0-89256-323-0

Published simultaneously in Canada by Collier Macmillan Canada, Inc.
Packaged by Rapid Transcript, a division of March Tenth, Inc.
Composition by Folio Graphics Co., Inc.
Designed by Christine Kettner
First Edition

TO MOTHER
whose unconditional love
is my most valued treasure

Do not be conformed to this world
but be transformed by the renewal of your mind.

ROMANS 12:2

CONTENTS

ACKNOWLEDGMENTS

I wish first of all to thank the thousands of readers of *Anxiety and Panic Attacks: Their Cause and Cure* for sharing with me, through calls and letters, their personal experiences with anxiety and panic attacks. Their stories, questions, and suggestions inspired the writing of this book.

The contribution of Pauline Neff, my co-author, is immeasurable. Her talent, patience, and sensitivity to those who suffer has given this book its heart. I also wish to express my gratitude to Cynthia Handly for her continuing support and editorial suggestions. Thanks also to Jim Wilson and Dr. Wayne Jones for their professional contributions.

I am especially indebted to Toni Sciarra and Eleanor Rawson for their editorial guidance.

Most important is my deepest appreciation to my wife Jane for sharing her love, truth, and spirituality and for reawakening the same in me.

PART

I

WHY YOU DON'T HAVE
TO BE AFRAID ANYMORE

CHAPTER

CHAPTER

1

THE PROMISE OF
BEYOND FEAR

S INCE THE PUBLICATION in 1985 of my first book, *Anxiety and Panic Attacks*, I have received a tremendous number of letters and phone calls. People who for years had been housebound with life-inhibiting fears and phobias wanted to tell me their good news: After reading my book and practicing the Five Basic Principles, they were able to venture to the store, ride in a car, go back to work, and feel better about themselves! One man even said that just reading the book gave him a "high" that lasted for several days and allowed him to function without the many fears that had dominated his life.

At the same time, some readers recognized that while they had improved, they needed some more help in overcoming irrational fears. "I can cope now," said a woman who had practiced my Five Basic Principles to overcome the panic attacks that had prevented her from living a normal life. "I can go out of the house, but I'd like to be able to take my daughter to lunch and enjoy it." Her goal was to rid herself *completely* of any residue of irrational fears.

Others said that they had realistic fears stemming from stressful events that had occurred in their lives, such as a divorce, loss of a job, or bad health. They wanted to know if the Five Basic Principles would work for rational as well as irrational fears.

In all the letters, I heard the same theme—people hungered to do more than just function at a subsistence level; they wanted what I call Life Plus, the ability to feel 100 percent good about themselves, enjoy life, and be able to help others at the same time. They wanted to go *beyond fear* to serenity, confidence, and happiness.

That is why I have written this book. *Beyond Fear* is for you, if you have a phobia; if you have learned to cope with a phobia but want to do more than just cope; if you have realistic fears; or even if you have that vague kind of fear, that empty feeling that you are not getting out of life everything you'd like. I know that you can have the Life Plus transformation that enabled me to find peace and happiness and freedom from fear.

What is Life Plus? It is being able to get in touch with your unconscious and use it as a tool to keep you free of anxiety no matter how many stress-producing events clutter your existence. It is mastering techniques that enable you to take control and change your faulty self-perceptions. It is becoming so attuned to your spiritual self that you know without a doubt that you love yourself and others without reservation. When you feel this good about yourself, you are not a prisoner to the doubts, fears, and insecurities you have had in the past. You desire and *dare* to reach out and help others.

Life Plus made me a different person, yet it was no guarantee against experiencing tough times, even failures. It was, however, the knowledge that it was really all right if I should risk some new endeavor and fail. Regardless of the fact that I got a divorce, floundered with uncertainty on turning 40, and struggled with the onslaughts of anxiety on becoming a public figure when sales of my first book rocketed, I was still OK because I could see these stress-producing events not as threats but as *challenges* for me to grow and develop more than I already had.

With Life Plus, I could love myself enough to avoid heart palpitations, choking fits, trembling, or that awful feeling that I was going to black out, curse, or otherwise make a fool of myself in public. I could feel healthy excitement instead of fear about making speeches, eating alone, flying in an airplane, driving over a bridge, or going to a shopping center. I didn't have to be afraid of what would happen to me if I risked ending a relationship or failing in business.

Now I find that I can apply Life Plus tools to irrational as well as rational fears. And so can you. You do not need to endure terrorizing panic attacks and debilitating anxiety over common, everyday actions that hold no danger in themselves. You don't need to fear success and limit your potential in your career or relationships, either. The problem for millions of fear-ridden Americans is not the podium, the plane, or the probability that a marriage will fail. After talking to readers of *Anxiety and Panic Attacks,* I am even more convinced that *the problem is fearing the way you will feel* while the stress-producing event is taking place.

I have developed Five FEAR-Smasher keys specifically designed to help you go *beyond fear.* By using these keys you can change from the inside out so that you can become what you may never have expected to be: a person who can live with life's stresses yet remain free of the physical symptoms of fear and *even attain new heights of happiness.*

My Promise to You

In *Beyond Fear,* I will show you all of the following:

- Ways to increase your commitment to overcoming fear
- The latest medical research on anxiety and panic disorder and the newest psychological tools for obliterating a multitude of specific fears
- Improved methods for reprogramming your unconscious so that it will help you do away with fear by increasing your self-esteem
- A complete program that makes it easy to put my five FEAR-Smasher keys to work and monitor your progress

I will also challenge you to take risks by giving examples of those who have failed and failed again and then gone on to succeed. And I will encourage you to use the greatest key of all, the sharing of the special talents that you are developing as you overcome your fears, so that you can help others with the same problem.

These are the keys that have worked for me. They have already given encouragement and hope to many with whom I have had contact. They can work for you, if you will use them. You, too, can have Life Plus.

2

UNDERSTANDING THE
FEAR SYNDROME

Dear Mr. Handly,

Thank you for sharing your own experiences in your loving and healing book, *Anxiety and Panic Attacks*. Last year I had to drop out of graduate school, but not because of poor grades. (I had made an A in every class I took the first semester.) The problem was that I had an overwhelming fear about my inability to speak in class. I was afraid, really afraid, of making a fool of myself. Somehow it seemed that if I spoke, I would be revealed for a fraud.

After reading your book, I realized I was a social phobic. I started practicing the Five Basic Principles you presented. Now I'm going back to school in the fall, and I believe I can speak up in class. But I'm still very afraid. Do you have any further advice for me? I need all the support and resources I can get.

THIS LETTER from a young man was typical of many I received after the publication of my first book, *Anxiety and Panic Attacks*. Readers told me how their irrational fears had once dominated them. They had believed themselves to be flawed or ill-fated. Some even feared they were going insane. Then they told me how practicing *Anxiety and Panic Attack's* Five Basic Principles helped them conquer their fear habits and gain a new perspective. They began to see themselves as the worthy persons they really were. They started to desensitize themselves to their fear by taking small and gradual steps to do the very thing they were afraid of. And they found they could do it!

For some, just being *hopeful* that they really could do something about their fear was a big step.

A 33-year-old whom I'll call Dorothy, the mother of two children, wrote me the following letter:

> I had my first panic attack when I was 27 while I was driving a car on a bridge. After that, I stopped driving. I sought psychiatric treatment, but still I could drive only if someone was in the car with me. In fact, I was frightened of having a panic attack if I had to do *anything* alone. I couldn't go anywhere where there were crowds of people because I felt so threatened. It was as if everyone was coming at me.
>
> After reading your book, I realize I'm afraid of fooling around with these panic attacks. If you can get over them, so can I. I'm willing to go to work, and I have a husband who backs me up 100 percent.

Dorothy has not only hope but also commitment. That's another important step toward going beyond fear to Life Plus.

Libby wrote to tell me that she has taken the most helpful step of all toward finding Life Plus: *action*. Having suffered anxiety and a "nervous stomach" for which her doctor was prescribing medication, Libby told me that she was in the process of desensitizing herself to her fears.

> It's hard work, but I am practicing your book's advice to tell myself that I am calm, confident, and functioning normally. This has helped me tremendously. In fact, I now see that I used to be just as you described yourself—passive, dependent, suspicious that people didn't like me, and worried about my health and future. I still have a lot of work to do, and I'm still not completely certain that I can do it, but I remind myself that *you changed and so can I!* Your book is an answer to my prayer.

Libby went on to tell me that she wanted a support group for herself so badly that she was organizing one herself. Despite her feelings of insecurity, she was using her new knowledge to *reach out to others*. By doing so, she felt more assured of her self-worth. She was taking another step forward on the path to Life Plus.

Would you, too, like to find Life Plus? Maybe you are one of the millions of people in the country who suffer from anxiety and panic attacks. According to a March 1986 report by psychiatrist James Reich in the *Journal of Nervous and Mental Disease*, 3 percent of the population in the United States experiences panic, 6 percent agoraphobia, 3 percent generalized anxiety, 2.5 percent simple phobias (fear of a specified situation, object, creature, activity, or experience), and 1.5 percent social phobias (dread of situations in which you may be observed by others in such acts as eating, speaking, writing, vomiting, or urinating). Research by the National Institute of Mental Health shows that phobias and related anxiety disorders are the *most common psychological problems* in America. Over 13 million people are affected.

If you have one of these problems, you are not alone. Like millions of others, you may have genetic differences that cause your body to react more sensitively to stress. You may have learned poor habits of coping with the stress in your life. But you can change! Fears, nervous symptoms, feelings of insecurity, psychosomatic illnesses, and depression do not have to dominate your life!

If you are not subject to anxiety and panic, thank your stars and read on. This book can be the pathway to Life Plus for you as well. Why do I say that? Because if you live in today's world, you live with stress. The tools that help anxious people cope with stress can help anyone who worries or feels afraid.

How Irrational Fears Changed My Life

Fear of success that diminishes your ability to achieve; guilt because you got a divorce or parented less than perfect children, anguish that comes from an inner voice that tells you you don't quite measure up—these emotions may not make your life as miserable as that of the agoraphobic who experiences outright terror, but they can still make you function below par. I know this from my own experience. At 33, before I had a panic attack, I looked like a winner but felt like a loser. Others saw me as a successful businessman with my own executive search firm. I had a better than average income, a loving wife named Cindy, and a beautiful home. We golfed and traveled. To hide my feelings of not deserving to be successful, however, I played the part of "good old Bob, the guy who loves to have fun" with my friends.

Looking back, I realize that I had a lot of anxieties I didn't even recognize as being stressful. I secretly dwelled on my failures, not on my successes. Everyone else seemed to be able to do anything better than I could. I felt like a fraud, and my body responded to my feelings. I had constant bouts of diarrhea, colitis, and a nervous stomach.

I'll never forget my first panic attack. Wham! One day as I sat in my office reading the *Wall Street Journal,* my heart suddenly began to pound. Perspiration broke out on my forehead. My stomach flopped over and my mind raced out of control. I felt as if I were going to black out.

That was the first panic attack, but it wasn't the last. I told my doctor I was having heart attacks, but he said there wasn't anything physically wrong with me and gave me tranquilizers. The pills reduced my anxiety but did nothing to stop the frightening attacks. Soon I began to avoid going to the places where I experienced panic. Finally I couldn't go anywhere. I was housebound.

Depression followed as my life, my career, and my hopes began to fade. Just as I was on the point of considering suicide as the only alternative, I read an article in a newspaper about a woman who had the same symptoms. The article said she had agoraphobia (a word I'd never heard) and that she was becoming normal again after being treated by a psychotherapist named Jim Wilson, of the Phobia Centers of the Southwest in Dallas. I lost no time in visiting Jim, who explained what had happened to me.

The Fear Habit Explained

Jim immediately began to teach me how to use behavioral tools that would help me overcome my agoraphobia. First, I learned that a panic attack was simply a "fight or flight" response—the body's normal way of preparing anyone to react efficiently to danger. Jim told me that in my case, my body perceived my inability to cope with stress as just such a danger—a threat that might require the fight-or-flight response.

"The body's ability to deal with stress is much like a rain barrel's capacity for holding water," Jim told me. "As the stress level begins to build, you experience *anticipatory anxiety*—your body becomes aroused to prepare to fight against the dangers you perceive in a stressful situation or to flee from it. Blood vessels in the surface areas of your body begin to constrict so that blood can be diverted deep within to supply your muscles. Your heart rate increases in order to rush fuel—oxygen-laden blood—to every cell. Salivary glands dry up in anticipation of the loss of fluids through perspiration. All functions not involved in fighting or fleeing, such as digestion, shut down to conserve energy."

Then Jim went on to explain that in today's civilized world, we usually can't fight or flee from our stressors, so the anxiety level continues to build. When it reaches the overflow point, our bodies call in their ultimate weapon: adrenaline, a hormone that within seconds compounds all the arousal symptoms tremendously. Even if you're just sitting in your office, as I was when my "rain barrel" reached the overflow point, you will have a panic attack because your body has signaled the adrenaline to flow. You may not recognize the symptoms as a fight-or-flight response because you don't see any concrete object to fear. The palpitations, dry mouth, nausea, and faintness may seem like a heart attack.

Even if you have panic attacks, you don't have a phobia until you start avoiding the place or situation in which you experienced the terrible symptoms. If your adrenaline begins to spurt while you are making a speech, while you are surrounded by strangers at the beach, or when you are driving on a bridge, you may become so frightened of the way your body feels that you avoid those activities. When you start avoiding things, you develop a phobia.

Just learning the truth about what caused my panic attacks did a lot toward helping me recover. Jim taught me the importance of relaxation. He also taught me how to desensitize myself to panic by gradually exposing myself to the places where the fears had developed. In order to be able to desensitize myself, he advised me to do cognitive restructuring—to replace my irrational, fearful thoughts about myself with positive, rational thoughts.

Then I embarked on my own self-improvement campaign. I read many books on how to improve my self-image. I took a course that taught me how to control the rate at which my brain cycled. Then I was able to reach a level of brain wave activity known as alpha (characterized by a sense of deep relaxation) so that I could program my unconscious to change the way I thought, felt, and reacted. I did this by using visualizations and affirmations, and soon my unconscious "boss" was helping me overcome my fears. I was so delighted with the improvements in myself that I began to set important physical, mental, and spiritual goals. I decided to lose weight, exercise for physical fitness, stop drinking, and make contact with my spiritual self.

After I learned these better ways of coping with stress, I completely overcame agoraphobia. I was able to travel to Europe, improve my business, even make speeches without feeling the slightest twinge of discomfort. But the greatest thing of all was a transformation experience that happened a few months after I put all of this into practice. As I rode with Cindy down the highway one afternoon listening to a self-improvement tape, I somehow suddenly *knew* that I could now love myself. My insecurity, my feelings of being a fraud, were all gone. I was certain that I could do anything I wanted with my life. Furthermore, I, who had always been so wrapped up in my own problems that I couldn't think of anyone else's, now wanted to reach out and help others. This new way to live was so wonderful that I started calling it Life Plus, because I not only had gotten my life back, but so much more in addition!

Genesis of the Five Basic Principles

After I attained Life Plus and discovered that I wanted to help other people overcome their fears and phobias, I collaborated with Pauline Neff to write *Anxiety and Panic Attacks*. We sifted through all the instruction Jim had given me, as well as my own research and the principles of positive thinking, and put everything together in Five Basic Principles that could be easily followed. Here they are:

Basic Principle Number One: "Use the creative powers of your unconscious mind to help you change yourself." With this tool, you can learn, as I did, that the unconscious is like a boss who causes you to be afraid even though you tell yourself consciously that you needn't be. The unconscious stores feelings, not rational thoughts, and makes you a prisoner of them. The good news is that the unconscious can be accessed by learning to relax in such a way that you cause your brain waves to cycle at the alpha level. While you are in this state, you can use simple techniques to retrain your unconscious. Thus your "boss" becomes an enlightened one who helps rather than hinders you.

Basic Principle Number Two: "Use visualizations and affirmations to change your self-image so that you feel confidence rather than fear." This principle teaches you how to reprogram your unconscious by going to alpha and affirming yourself with positive statements and visualizations. You visualize yourself behaving in positive rather than negative ways. By doing this, you can actually "transfuse" positive feelings into your subconscious system.

Basic Principle Number Three: "Use rational and positive thinking to see yourself and events as they really are and also to visualize how you want them to be." Mastering this principle enables you to refuse to answer the phone when Mr. Negative (all your self-doubts and poor self-esteem) calls. You do this through cognitive restructuring—a process of examining the irrational thoughts that have created a poor self-image and replacing them with rational, positive ones.

Basic Principle Number Four: "Act as if you are already the way you want to be." This process means that you intentionally act *as if* you already had a good self-image and were free of fear. The acting *as if* principle enables you to retrain your unconscious and also to embark on the desensitization process that is basic to overcoming irrational fears.

Basic Principle Number Five: "Set goals to become the person you want to be." This principle teaches you how to set short-term goals as an easy way of reaching long-term ones. By setting and mastering positive goals for physical, mental, and spiritual improvement, you not only overcome irrational fears but may also have a transformation experience as I did when I found Life Plus.

These Five Basic Principles were the rationale for my book, *Anxiety and Panic Attacks.* These are the principles that have already helped so many people suffering from irrational fears to recover and go on to a life of happiness and fulfillment.

How Life Plus Kept the Fear Out of Divorce

At the same time that I was writing my first book, I also embarked on a new career as a professional speaker. With the book's success came many speaking engagements across the country, and I began to take my fear-breaking message to more and more people.

I was thrilled with the fact that I really was helping other people overcome the fears and phobias in their lives. I enjoyed the good feelings that Life Plus brought me. But I soon discovered that Life Plus wasn't going to render me immune to stress or to life events that would make most people feel negative, defeated, and afraid.

Here is what happened to me after I found Life Plus. My

marriage broke up. I turned 40 and had to deal with all the anxiety and self-examination that that birthday brings for many people. I pursued a career in which I had to overcome the number one fear in America—that of public speaking. Even the success of having a best-selling book, with the attendant television and other public appearances, was destined to cause stress.

I'll never forget the devastating feeling I had on the terrible day that I discovered that Cindy did not love me, and, in fact, felt that she never had. For fifteen years, we had had a sharing, caring marriage. I had worshiped, even adored Cindy. I believed that my life in the future would be one in which we lived in Dallas, pursued our separate careers, and lived happily ever after. In one terrible moment, I discovered that I had lost everything. I was in shock for about two weeks. I reacted with anger, hurt, disappointment, and despair. I felt as low as I had when I was housebound with agoraphobia.

Yet because I had Life Plus, my self-esteem remained strong enough for me to talk to Cindy. I began to understand that she was telling me her honest feelings. I saw that what she was saying didn't really have anything to do with me. I wasn't a failure. I wasn't unlovable. The feelings were hers, not mine.

While Cindy tried counseling, I began to implement the tools I had learned in getting over my agoraphobia. I went to my alpha level and reprogrammed my unconscious so that I could be in control of my thoughts. I visualized and affirmed myself as being lovable and capable of dealing with my life. Gradually, as I saw that divorce would be inevitable, I made goals for what my reaction would be. I visualized my life as I wanted it to be separate from Cindy. I visualized and affirmed myself adjusting, being happy and successful, meeting other people, dating and doing positive things that would help me create a new life. I acted *as if* I were already living and feeling that way. At the same time, I programmed myself to be able to love and accept Cindy no matter what decisions she made. When the divorce did go through, I was already beginning to adjust. Cindy and I severed our relationship without a lot of lawyers or a hostile court proceeding. We remained friends. We are still in touch frequently. I have also achieved my long-term goal of being able to share my life in a loving lasting relationship with someone.

How Life Plus Pulled Me Through a Mid-life Crisis

Even when life is going along as expected, the specter of a fortieth birthday causes most people to stop and ask, "Is this where I need to be? Is this where I want to be? Is this where I should be?" My life certainly was not going along as expected, because I was going through a divorce.

For many people, turning 40 is the time to set new goals to replace the ones you haven't reached. It's a time of taking new directions. I had taken a new direction, as I changed my career from that of executive headhunter to public speaker with a message for other people.

All these changes translated into a lot of stress that could have made me feel fearful and anxious. Here I was, on the point of a divorce. I had the stress of appearing on TV shows such as Phil Donahue's and on radio to talk about my book and keep it selling strongly. In my new career I was having to compete with better-established speakers.

If I hadn't already found Life Plus, I honestly think I would have destroyed myself. I would have been telling myself that because of the divorce I was a failure, a no-good, and a fraud. I'm not implying that I was free of self-doubt. Sure, the negative thoughts plagued me. But when they did, I had the self-esteem and the cognitive restructuring tools that enabled me to challenge them, see them as irrational, and take the responsibility for changing them. And I had skills that helped me translate these rational, positive thoughts into constructive behavior.

As for the stresses that came with promoting a best-selling book, I sailed through them without the nervous stomach and panicky feelings I had once had. When I was to appear on the Phil Donahue show, I felt the tingle of anxiety that anyone would feel on speaking before a national audience. But this tingle only added to my feeling of excitement at being able to reach so many more people. I experienced stress, but I could use that extra kick of adrenaline to do a better job rather than let it cause nervousness.

That is why I am convinced that the tools that helped me overcome agoraphobia also helped me maintain success while I was functioning as a "normal" person undergoing stress. That is why I have expanded the Five Basic Principles and formulated the five FEAR-Smasher keys. If you have panic, these keys will give you additional tools that will enable you to go beyond coping to enjoying life. If you don't have panic, they still can open up new avenues of self-fulfillment, no matter what problems life may have in store for you.

The FEAR-Smasher Keys

Here are the FEAR-Smasher keys:

F stands for "*First* take the responsibility for understanding your fear and changing your attitude toward it." You don't have to be a victim. When you take responsibility for your thoughts, you can make yourself what you want to be.

E stands for "*Establish* your self-worth." Self-confidence, which you win through achieving, is not the same thing as self-worth, which is the ability to love yourself no matter what you achieve. This key will help you perceive yourself in new and exciting ways through using self-nurturing techniques and increasing your awareness of the loving spiritual power within you.

A stands for "*Alpha*-program yourself to be free of fear and deserving of self-worth." Learn improved techniques for reaching the state of relaxation known as alpha. Learn new ways of visualizing and affirming serenity and happiness for yourself.

R stands for "*Risk* developing your ability to attempt new things." Trying and failing the first time, or any number of times, does not mean that you give up. When you have mastered this key, you will know that failure is sometimes a necessary preliminary to growth and success and that it does not affect your self-worth.

S stands for "*Share* the hope by reaching out to help others." There is therapeutic value in using the experience you gain in overcoming your own fears to help others do the same thing. If you really use this key, your self-esteem and spiritual awareness will soar. You will be better equipped to face life's stresses and your own rational and irrational fears.

Outwitting the Wolves and Witches

Because fear is such a universal experience, many childhood fairy tales deal with the subject of being afraid. These much loved stories teach us that big, bad wolves and wicked witches *can* be conquered, that if we take appropriate action, we can do away with villains. When we believe in our power to do this, we no longer have to be afraid.

My FEAR-Smasher keys can work for you in much the same way. Because they have been proved to work, you can *believe* that it is possible for you to recover from a phobia and *banish* your fear forever.

To help you master the keys, I will teach you techniques that have been devised by professionals who help people successfully combat fears and phobias. In later chapters I will share the exciting new research that has been done on specific kinds of phobias. I will combine all of this in the FEAR-Smasher keys so they will be easy for you to use.

Your first steps in learning to use the FEAR-Smashers are these:

1. Buy a loose-leaf or spiral notebook.
2. Reserve a section for each of the five keys. Plan to write down how you, as an individual, can practice the keys in your life.
3. Leave a large section marked "Journal."

First Assignment

Before continuing with the next chapter, write down in your journal what you hope to achieve in gaining Life Plus. You may want to use these starter sentences:

1. I want to overcome the fear of _____.
2. I want to feel _____.
3. I want to understand why _____.
4. I want to be able to _____.
5. I want to give up _____.

My Approach to Stopping Fear

My approach to coping with stress and fears and arriving at Life Plus is a holistic one. I am firmly convinced that we can use our body, mind, and spirit to go beyond fear. Many experts believe that other approaches are best. In fact, for anyone who has fears, the wide choice of therapies presented may only increase the level of stress. In the next chapter, I will detail several of the latest recommended therapies and explore the advantages of my holistic approach.

Meanwhile, reward yourself by doing something especially nice for yourself today. By reading to this point, you have taken the first step, which says, "I care about myself enough to invest some time in my recovery." You are on your way to the wonderful adventure of Life Plus.

3

WHAT WORKS AND WHAT DOESN'T

APPLAUSE BROKE OUT when Dr. Alan Francis, a professor of psychiatry from Cornell University, made this observation before the Seventh Annual National Conference on Phobias and Related Anxiety Disorders:

> [For phobias] there are several different biological treatments, a number of cognitive and behavioral methods, a number of psychodynamic treatments, and I have treated patients with each of these and gotten good results with all of them. . . . What do we [professionals with differing viewpoints] do? . . . We're not engaged in a horse race, trying to find out which treatment is best. The much more interesting question is to determine the specificity of actions that make the most sense—which treatment for which patient under which circumstance is most attractive.

The audience, made up of phobics and the professionals who treat them, applauded for two reasons. First, these people knew only too well about the conflict among the scientific disciplines used to help phobics recover. And they also knew from experience that a treatment that works for one person doesn't always work for another. A "package" of various treatments from which to select, rather than a single one, seemed like the solution.

If you are a fearful person who is trying to overcome a phobia or a fear on your own, the wealth of treatment avenues open to you may be confusing. You hear talk of "in vivo exposure," "cognitive/behavioral therapies," "psycho-analysis," or "neurolinguistic programming,"—code words for various kinds of therapies that mean nothing to the lay person.

You may want a doctor to prescribe a drug that will block your fear, but you may be uncertain about which drug is best. Or you may be radically opposed to the use of drugs and want to be sure that the therapist you choose will not insist that you use them.

If these are your thoughts, to which professional do you go? If you want to free yourself of phobias and fears on your own, whose tools are the most effective?

Since even professionals disagree about which treatment is best, you should know about the full range of options. What are the odds of recovery for each? What are the advantages and disadvantages? Once you learn about the treatment tools that therapists use, you may want to try to use some of them yourself. If you don't feel you are progressing on your own, you may want to select a therapist. If you have read this took and are informed about the choices you have, you will be able to ask the questions that will lead you to the therapist best able to help you.

Many enlightened therapists inform their clients of various treatment options, but some do not. Moreover, some doctors, psychiatrists, and psychologists lack training in how best to address the special problems faced by phobics. In my opin-ion, a well-trained therapist who has recovered from some kind of phobia and who uses the treatment you prefer would be ideal.

This chapter will pose the questions you may be wanting to ask about treatment options. I'll give you the latest findings on the subject of overcoming fear.

The Options Market

I don't understand why there isn't a definitive best way to treat phobias and fears. Can you tell my why?

Options in phobia treatment today seem almost as numerous as the options available for trading on the stock market. They don't fluctuate in value quite as quickly, but the consensus among treatment professionals about what works does change from year to year.

One reason for this is that a phobia is a combination of physical, mental, and emotional problems. Some people are just born physiologically more sensitive to fear. It takes less of a threat to trigger their brain to send adrenaline coursing through the bloodstream. At the same time, because of childhood influences, they may be unprepared emotionally to cope with stress in positive ways. These inappropriate reactions to stress lead to minor or major illnesses, such as ulcers, headaches, colitis, nervous stomach, and high blood pressure.

Therapies for treating phobias cover psychoanalytic, behavioral, cognitive, and biological levels. Each treatment reflects a different belief about the cause of phobias and consequently a different way to overcome them.

The Psychiatric Options

What are the options that psychiatry offers in the treatment of phobias?

Psychoanalytic treatment began with Freud in 1905 and is still the choice of psychoanalytic psychiatrists. It is based on the theory that people become phobic when they try to repress a childhood desire or a feeling that they believe is sinful or wrong, such as a sexual attraction to the parent of the opposite sex. Or, as adults, they may be overwhelmed by "global anxiety"—a great deal of real or imagined stress such as that felt after the death of a loved one or when job security is threatened. Fearing that they will become detached from reality, these people protect themselves by focusing their anxiety away from the stressful loss or the repressed desire and placing it instead on a bridge, an elevator, or a cat. By substituting a less threatening inanimate object or an animal for the real concern, they reduce the amount of fear they feel. And because they can control the fear by simply avoiding the phobic place or animal, they feel more secure. Originally, psychoanalytic treatment for phobics was a lengthy process of exploring the past to discover the repressed childhood desire or the actual cause of global anxiety. Patients often gained a better understanding of themselves and thus could relate better to other people. Often, however, they did not recover from their phobias.

Now there is growing recognition among analysts that cognitive and behavioral treatments are more effective at helping patients recover from phobias. At the same time, psychoanalytic treatments will benefit patients who have personality problems or recurring interpersonal or situational conflicts that create stress and exacerbate anxiety. Some psychiatrists now advocate a special kind of psychoanalysis that is as short as three to four months for phobic patients. After that period of time, the patient and psychiatrist can assess the results and decide whether lengthier treatment is required.

The Behavioral Option

What is meant by behavioral psychology, and how does it differ from psychoanalytic psychiatry?

Behavioral forms of treatment began as early as the 1920s when John B. Watson, the founder of the behavioral movement in psychology, proved that people could be conditioned to be afraid of objects that in themselves were not dangerous. For instance, Watson conditioned "little Albert" to fear his pet rat by causing the child to associate a frightening noise with the rat. Each time the clinician gave Albert his pet rat, he also struck a metal bar with a hammer. The loud noise was so frightening to the little boy that it brought tears. Soon Albert cried whenever he saw the rat, even though the noise was eliminated.

In like manner, Watson held that phobics are conditioned to

their irrational fears because they associate a frightening experience with a specific place, object, or situation. For instance, if as a child you were afraid to be left at the day care center, and each time you arrived a certain song was played on the record player, you might for no apparent reason have a panic attack when you heard that song as an adult. You could learn to fear dogs after being bitten by one. You could become phobic about driving a car after a bad accident. Post-traumatic stress disorder, suffered by war veterans and victims of rape or childhood abuse, is such a form of conditioning.

Behaviorists liken phobias to bad habits. They believe that if you can be conditioned to fear dogs or driving in cars, you can also be deconditioned by establishing new associations with the object of your fear. One of these behavioral techniques is *systematic desensitization,* a process of reducing the intensity of your fear by approaching and then entering the feared situation in graduated steps. Eventually you become acclimated, and the fear is gone. For instance, if you are phobic of dogs, you might use *imaginal desensitization* by imagining that you were first approaching, then petting, and finally picking up a dog. Or, as is now considered more efficient, you would practice *in vivo* or *exposure desensitization.* Accompanied by a therapist, you first approach a puppy, pet it, pick it up, and then go on to pet an older dog. The therapist rewards you with praise each time you enter the feared situation. As you learn to cope with the fear you feel at each step, you eventually decondition yourself to the fear response.

Exposure is the one treatment that most professional disciplines agree is a must in treating phobias. Research has shown that in vivo exposure is superior to imaginal desensitization. I desensitized myself to my fear of leaving my safe place, and you can practice this kind of therapy on your own with any situation that causes anxiety. Or, if desired, you can choose a therapist who will lead you through an eight- to twenty-week program of group therapy and individual in vivo exposure.

One way in which therapists combine psychiatry and in vivo therapy is through *contextual therapy,* as originated by psychiatrist Manuel D. Zane, who founded one of the first phobia clinics in the United States at the White Plains Medical Hospital Center in White Plains, New York. The psychiatrist helps phobics explore the role played by their thoughts, feelings, expectations, and imagery in combination with their outer social and physical environments. Therapists accompany phobics as they expose themselves to the feared situation and help them recognize the difference between the dangers imagined and ones that are real. These techniques are also advocated by Dr. Claire Weekes, the Australian who pioneered the idea of teaching lay people to use exposure methods for themselves; Dr. Isaac Marks, a noted British researcher in the field of phobias; and Dr. Arthur B. Hardy, founder of TERRAP (for "territorial apprehensiveness"), a program of group and individual phobia treatment available in many U.S. cities.

Another behavioral technique is one called *flooding, ungraded exposure,* or *implosion therapy.* This is an attempt to exorcise the fear by imagining and then experiencing the worst possible scenario. For instance, patients who are afraid of heights are encouraged to imagine themselves falling from the top of a fifty-story building. Then, in one fell swoop, the therapist takes them immediately to the top of such a building. Although this "white knuckle" approach to desensitization works for some people, many therapists believe that a more gradual approach is better.

Behaviorists also use *paradoxical intention* to reassure clients that their worst fears of becoming totally overwhelmed by their symptoms will not come true. In this technique, phobics attempt to maximize the frightening physical symptoms of fear rather than trying to alleviate them. Paradoxically, they find that when they try to conjure up their fear symptoms, the intensity of the symptoms is reduced.

Biology and Behavioral Psychology

But if phobias are partially caused by physical conditions, how does behavioral psychology help in that respect?

Though no researcher has proved that phobias and fear

result from a physical condition, there is evidence that indicates phobics are abnormal in their physiological sensitivity. The locus ceruleus in the brain stem contains 70 percent of the noradrenaline in the brain and is thought to be the main control center for the fight-or-flight response. If you inherit an oversensitivity in this center, you experience the emergency response more frequently than a person whose brain is not overly sensitive. For instance, loud noises may only startle the normal person. For you, they might be the cause of a panic attack.

Recognizing that it is a physical impossibility for the body to be relaxed and tense at the same time, behavioral psychologists advocate *relaxation training*. They teach *diaphragmatic breathing*, clenching and releasing of muscles, and body therapy as ways of reducing the physical reactions of a fight-or-flight response. (I will explain these methods in more detail in later chapters.)

Fitness routines and a sensible program of regular exercise can also help fear-prone people maintain calm and overcome the psychosomatic illnesses associated with anxiety, such as tension and migraine headaches, ulcers, high blood pressure, nervous stomach, colitis, and low back pain.

Behavioral psychologists advocate better nutrition not only to make you healthier but also because some substances in our foods have been shown to contribute to anxiety. Sugar may make you hyperactive. Caffeine is especially harmful, since it stimulates the adrenal glands to emit anxiety-causing hormones. Alcohol may cause you to feel better temporarily but leave you less able to deal with the anxiety after its effect wears off. Also on the behavioral psychologists' forbidden list is nicotine, since it is anxiety-stimulating.

Other physical problems associated with the fear-prone are mitral valve prolapse, hypoglycemia, hyperthyroidism, inner ear disturbances, and anemia. Behaviorists might recommend that you see your doctor to alleviate these conditions.

The Cognitive Option

What does the cognitive form of psychology have to offer?

The *cognitive* explanation of phobias holds that your faulty self-image, acquired through what you tell yourself about yourself, causes your fears. Frightening feelings, negative daydreams, and fear-producing self-talk are some of the cognitions that produce a faulty self-image. To improve your self-image, you must first find out what these faulty cognitions are, decide rationally that they are false, and finally *restructure* the thought in a positive way.

For instance, you might feel that you "can't" make a speech because your throat would close up, and then you would look foolish and people who saw you in this humiliating condition would reject you. If so, your cognitive goal would be to identify these fears. Then you would consider the reality of the situation—that even if you did not speak as well as you would have liked, you are still a person of worth; that people are not likely to reject you because you experience this very common fear, and that even if they did, there are still plenty of people who like you. You would then make affirming statements about yourself, such as "I am a person of worth" or "There are plenty of people who like me," and repeat these statements to yourself to overcome the anticipatory anxiety of speaking.

The cognitive school of thought, of which Dr. Aaron Beck is the leading exponent today, holds that it is what you perceive about yourself, not the reality of the situation, that causes phobias. If you change your self-perceptions, you will be free of fear.

The Medication Option

Aren't there drugs that can control panic attacks?

In the mid-1960s, Dr. Donald Klein of Columbia Medical Center discovered that panic attacks could be prevented by the tricyclic antidepressant imipramine (Tofranil). Since then, medication has been another option for persons who have panic attacks. Researchers have now proved that the locus ceruleus in the brain, which is thought to be responsible for the fight-or-flight response, can be controlled with medication in two ways. Benzodiazepines increase the activity of the inhibitor, GABA, which psychologists like Jim Wilson refer to as the "natural tranquilizer." Tricyclic antidepressants and another major antidepressant family, the monoamine oxidase inhibitors (MAOs), are thought to inhibit panic attacks while elevating the depressed mood that goes along with them.

Benzodiazepines currently being prescribed include alprozalam (Xanax) and clonazepam (Klonopin). Xanax is still the drug of choice, because of its fast action and fewer side effects. Research has proved that it does block panic attacks, immediately in some cases and within three to four days in others. Taken sublingually (under the tongue), it blocks panic in five to ten minutes. To avoid its main side effect, sedation, physicians start with the lowest possible dose, increasing it only as the patient tolerates or needs it. The average effective dose is 6 milligrams per day. Another side effect is drug dependence, which may occur after several months. Patients who want to stop taking Xanax without suffering withdrawal effects must gradually reduce the dosage rather than quit abruptly. Yet psychiatrists say that it does not, like many addictive substances, cause a craving for more and more of the drug. When it is time to eliminate Xanax, the physican tapers off the dose over a period of time in order to prevent physical discomfort.

Although Klonopin has the highest affinity for the GABA receptor and does block panic attacks, patients are subject to the side effects of drowsiness and headache more often than with Xanax. There is evidence that another benzodiazepine, lorazepam (Ativan), also has an affinity for the GABA receptor, but to be effective the dose might have to be as high as 20 milligrams per day.

In the past, many physicians prescribed diazepam (Valium) for panic attacks, but now it is believed that a mammoth dose of 80 milligrams per day would be necessary to do any good. No research has shown that Valium at any dose is effective.

Clonodine (Catapres), a type of blood pressure medication, works as a direct inhibitor of the cells in the locus ceruleus, but its effectiveness to block panic lasts for only a few days to a few weeks at most.

Among the tricyclic antidepressants that clearly suppress panic attacks are imipramine (Tofranil), desipramine (Norpramin), and nortriptylline (Pamelor). Maprotiline (Ludiomil) and amitriptyline (Elavil) are also thought to be effective. Although doxepin (Sinequan) and trazedone (Desyrel) are also prescribed when all else has failed, no research clearly demonstrates their effectiveness.

Tricyclics may require three to four weeks before producing a significant effect. Their side effects include an increased heart rate, dizziness, dry mouth, and occasionally a slight blurring of vision. To minimize side effects, physicians start the tricyclics at low dosages, increasing dosages if needed and if the patient tolerates the medication. Physicians may also prescribe a combination of benzodiazepines and tricyclics to minimize side effects. In this case, the physician tapers off the benzodiazepines before the patient becomes dependent on them.

The MAO inhibitors Nardil and Parnate are now being prescribed mostly to reduce anticipatory anxiety—the bodily arousal that occurs just by thinking about having to face a stressful place or situation. Because MAOs elevate depressed mood and increase confidence, they help reduce the "what if" thinking that produces anticipatory anxiety. Usually 150 to 300 milligrams is required. Patients on MAOs must follow dietary restrictions to avoid high blood pressure and severe headache. Other side effects include sleep difficulties, increased appetite, orgasmic dysfunction, drowsiness, and dry mouth.

The beta blockers Inderal and Tenormin are prescribed for social phobias. By partially blocking beta-adrenergic receptors and thus lessening the effects of adrenaline, these drugs reduce the anticipatory anxiety that creates physical arousal immediately before stressful encounters. They must be taken about one hour before such an encounter.

Ask doctors who routinely prescribe medication for panic attacks why they do so and they will say that research has proved that these drugs do physically block panic. They readily concede that research proves that in vivo exposure methods are the most effective behavioral/cognitive therapy but counter with the fact that no research can *prove* that such desensitization methods block fear as medications do. Still, that doesn't mean that phobics can't recover without drugs. After all, I did! So have a lot of others.

Few doctors believe that drugs alone will "cure" panic attacks. However, medication can block the fear that prevents some patients from being willing to participate in exposure therapy. For that reason, many doctors routinely prescribe drugs *before* beginning cognitive, behavioral, or psychoanalytical therapies. They use drug therapy as *one part* of a total therapeutic program.

In my opinion, there are some disadvantages to using drugs alone to recover from fears and phobias. Who wants to be dependent on drugs for the rest of their lives? Many agoraphobics are young women of childbearing age, and not enough research has been done to prove these drugs harmless to the fetus. Doctors say that while using drugs, patients avoid the relapses into panic that would cause demoralization. However, the relapse rate is high after drugs are discontinued if you haven't learned coping tools as well.

I believe that you should try to find a therapist who will work with you first without medication. If you find that you just cannot participate in exposure therapy without it, make a contract with the therapist that you will phase it out after a stated period of time. It is all too easy to become dependent on drugs and not ever fully recover from your phobia.

Because I recovered completely without the use of drugs, I believe that many of my readers can, too. If you should suffer a relapse into panic, you still do not have to go back to square one. Once you have mastered behavioral and cognitive techniques, you have effective tools to help you become panic-free once more. You can look on a relapse much as you would a sore throat that you got three years after getting over another sore throat. You don't have to feel guilty or depressed about it. You just go to work getting over the latest attack. Meanwhile, you don't have to put up with the disadvantages of medications.

If you learn to depend on drugs to control panic, you may not truly master the cognitive and behavioral tools you need in order to overcome panic. In my opinion, you run a greater risk of becoming demoralized over a relapse if you depend on medications, because you have nothing to fall back on but more drugs.

What if I have tried very hard to use cognitive/behavioral treatment but still have panic attacks?

If you really have tried and have experienced no improvement, you may need to use medications. Psychologist Jim Wilson of the Phobia Centers of the Southwest in Dallas believes that patients who are undergoing treatment should improve each week. If there is no improvement, he refers his client to Dr. Wayne Jones, a Dallas psychiatrist and medical director of the Phobia Centers, for drug treatment while continuing outpatient care. If the patient does not achieve a complete remission of all symptoms at some point, hospitalization at the Phobia Centers' inpatient facility is considered.

"Hospital treatment is also indicated when patients are unable to leave their home to attend outpatient programs or when extreme stress in the home situation sabotages progress," said Dr. Jones. "Our program includes daily assessment of medication, individual and group behavioral treatment and psychotherapy as needed. The average stay is two to four weeks, though patients who require the MAO inhibitors or who have a complicating medical or psychiatric condition may need to be hospitalized as long as eight weeks. Using this combined form of treatment, no patient at the inpatient facility has been a treatment failure. Most get completely well."

Dr. Jones believes that many patients who would respond to behavioral/cognitive treatment in six months could be treated simultaneously with drugs and become functional within two weeks in an inpatient facility and within six weeks on an outpatient basis. They could be off of medication within six months, he believes.

The Miscellaneous Options

Are any other options open to me?

Yes, there certainly are. Some of these are legitimate. Others are equivalent to trying to cure athlete's foot with bat's entrails. Let's discuss some of the newest treatments.

Neurolinguistic programming (NLP) is a technique that produces a semihypnotic state in order to help you dissociate yourself from your fear. The theory is that once you distance yourself from your phobia, you will be free of it forever. In NLP therapy, a professional might help you to relax and visualize a time when you felt completely relaxed and at ease. You would be taught to "play the movie" of this experience and enjoy all its emotions in your mind. Then the therapist would "anchor" this experience in your subconscious by touching you on your arm or leg. Next, you would play the movie of the earliest memory you have of feeling afraid of the situation you fear. The therapist would then touch your arm to release the good feelings that were anchored in, and the physical symptoms of fear that you normally experience when thinking of your phobic situation would be gone. Pioneered by psychologist Richard Bandler, M.A., and John Grinder, Ph.D. in linguistics, NLP seems to work well for some people. You can undergo therapy by a professional trained in NLP or attend courses that will help you practice this therapy on your own.

Hypnotic suggestion is used by some therapists in an attempt to help people overcome phobias. Hypnosis may be a good way to overcome the anticipatory anxiety that might prevent you from participating in desensitization, but it has been less successful in actually overcoming phobias.

Harold N. Levinson, M.D., of the New York University Medical Center, believes that *inner ear dysfunction* causes most phobias. He includes the locus ceruleus as a part of the inner ear system and advocates treatment with medications (including Xanax and Tofranil) that target this site. His theories (outlined in his book *Phobia-Free: A Medical Breakthrough*) are radically different from those of most physicians and other licensed professionals who treat phobias. While some people who suffer from inner ear dysfunction may have attendant panic attacks as a result, in my opinion, Dr. Levinson's theory that *most* phobias result from inner ear problems needs more research.

A *spiritual approach* to overcoming phobias can be found in groups that are similar to Alcoholics Anonymous. According to the professionals, this approach works, sometimes without additional therapy. Such groups include Emotions Anonymous and Agoraphobics in Motion (see "Where to Get Help and More Information" at the end of this book).

Support: An Important Option

How important is it to have the support of others?

Whether or not you use a therapist, you should seek out people who will support you as you attempt to overcome your fear. Ideal others might be a member of your family, a good friend, or a support group.

A good support person who is knowledgeable about fear, either through reading books or through special training, can encourage you to desensitize yourself. A group made up of other fearful people who have experienced what you have can have a powerful effect for good if the group is a positive one. I'll have more to say in future chapters about how you can get such support.

Are You Majoring or Minoring in Fear?

Now that I know there are several approaches to treating fears, I am more confused than ever. How do I know which kind of therapy I should pursue?

Here is a quiz to help you determine whether your problem is physical, interpersonal, psychiatric, or phobic:

1. Has a physical exam revealed that you are in good health and do not suffer from such disabilities as mitral valve prolapse, hypoglycemia, hyperthyroidism, or anemia? If so, it is likely that your fear symptoms can be reduced by your own efforts or by attending a phobia clinic or treatment center or by entering therapy with a psychiatrist or psychologist. If not, you may need to work with a competent physician to see if the treatment of the physical problem will help eliminate the fear disturbance. Be aware, however, that many physicians are not knowledgeable about the emotional causes of some physical problems. You may need both a doctor and a therapist.

2. Are you suffering from a major sleep disturbance? (Do you have severe insomnia, or do you sleep much more than you should?) If so, your problem could be depression, and you may need psychological attention along with phobia treatment.

3. Do you feel demoralized because you can't do the things you used to before you had a phobia? Once again, if the answer is yes, you may be suffering depression. It is normal for phobics to feel discouraged, even to contemplate suicide. If you feel truly depressed, if you have stopped enjoying the things that you would enjoy if you were not afraid, and if you have lost even the will to do the things you used to enjoy, seek treatment for depression first.

How to Ask Informed Questions

What kinds of questions should I ask a therapist before beginning treatment?

The Phobia Society of America states that good therapists will welcome your questions about treatment. It suggests finding out the following things about any form of treatment you are considering:

- What is the basic approach to treatment? Does it involve in vivo exposure? Is medication available?
- What additional kinds of treatment are available?
- Does the standard course of treatment have a fixed length? How long? Are there provisions for follow-up?
- What are the phobia-related training and experiences of the therapists? How long have they been treating people with phobias?
- What is the operative definition of success for the treatment program? Based on that definition, what is the program's rate of success?
- How much does the treatment cost? Is any of it reimbursable by your health insurance? Are there program graduates you could speak with?

The FEAR-Smasher Way to Overcome Phobias

Do I really need to work with a therapist, or can I cope with my fears on my own?

That is up to you. Since studies show that exposure therapy is most valuable, and this is a therapy you can do on your own or with a supportive lay person, you may be able to desensitize yourself. At any rate, I believe you will want to try to recover on your own. Only if it seems too difficult may you want to consult a therapist.

Now that you've explained all the different kinds of therapies, I wouldn't know where to begin. What can I do?

Don't worry if all this information seems overwhelming to you. I formulated the five FEAR-Smasher keys to make it easy for you to practice the therapies that are most valuable to you. In addition, my FEAR-Smasher keys include a powerful weapon that many professionals do not use—the ability of the unconscious mind to change your self-image and to allow you to feel good and confident about yourself.

Professionals tell us that all phobias can be cured. Whatever approach you choose, you should begin to see progress. If you do not, choose one of the other options. Also consider the possibility that if you are not making progress, you could perhaps be choosing to stay phobic. In that case, psychotherapy may prove beneficial.

Whether you use my FEAR-Smashers alone to help you recover or whether you use them in conjunction with a therapist, my experience tells me that they will help put you on a path to a full recovery.

4

My Fourteen-Day Plan for Using the FEAR-Smashers

W HEN ARCHITECTS design a multistory building, they may create what is known as a critical path, a plan which for maximum efficiency coordinates the purchasing of materials with the scheduling of work performed by the various contractors and engineers who lay the foundation, install the heating and air conditioning, and erect the building frame. A chart shows exactly when the supplies for each task will arrive and when each crew of workers will begin.

For you to build a calm new you as soon as possible, I have created what I call my Fourteen-Day Plan. It will tell you exactly when and how to start using each FEAR-Smasher key. I have also created a Daily Monitor and a Two-Month Monitor, which you can use to check whether you are using all of the keys most efficiently.

If you follow the Fourteen-Day Plan, which I outline below, you can be free of some of your anxiety and panic symptoms within the space of two short weeks. You can make a good start toward recovery. Here is what you can do:

Days One and Two: Read this book from cover to cover.

Day Three: Write in your log book some simple, easily attainable goals for yourself, such as these:

1. I will reread some part of *Beyond Fear* every day.
2. I will write in my journal every day.
3. I will tell other people that I am going to get over my fears by using the FEAR-Smashers.

Day Four: Paste blue dots in strategic places (see Chapter 6), and monitor your negative thoughts about yourself. Write these thoughts in your journal, and restructure them rationally.

Day Five: Create some simple affirmations, and write them in your journal, for instance:

1. I am a worthy person who deserves to be free of fear.
2. I am feeling calmer and happier every day.
3. I am using the FEAR-Smasher keys, and they are helping me.

Day Six: Buy a cassette tape and record the Alpha Script provided in Chapter 7. Plan your visualization of your secret resting place. Start thinking about who you want your support person to be. If you have an excellent prospect, ask this person if he or she is willing to help you. Have your support person read *Beyond Fear.* If you aren't sure who would be best, write in your journal the pros and cons of each prospect. Set a goal to ask someone to help you within the next three days.

Days Seven and Eight: Practice going to alpha six times a day if you are housebound, three times a day if you hold a job. When you attain the alpha state, relax in your secret resting place for fifteen minutes. Continue to write in your journal your negative thoughts and how you restructure them (Chapter 6).

Day Nine: Start using affirmations and visualizations to reprogram yourself against feeling fear while you are in alpha (Chapter 7).

Day Ten: Continue reprogramming at alpha. Start writing your hierarchy of fears (as listed in Chapter 8). Write down goals for beginning to desensitize yourself to your specific fears. Discuss these with your support person.

Days Eleven through Fourteen: Start desensitizing with the help of your support person. Write about your experiences in your journal, and give yourself an "attaboy" or "attagirl" for each attempt.

Using the Daily Monitor to Check Your Progress

Monitoring yourself not only assures you that you are using the FEAR-Smashers most efficiently; it also enables you to see how much progress you have made in banishing fear. Each success will make it easier for you to risk using the keys at a deeper level.

My Daily Monitor includes questions and affirmations that you can use at various times:

- In the morning before facing the day
- At midday to see how you're doing
- Before any event that's going to cause you some anxiety
- At night before bedtime to affirm how well you did and to consider some things you need to work on

These questions and affirmations will be different for everyone, since all of us have different fears and needs. However, here are some suggestions:

MORNING

- What action will I take today to work on overcoming fear? (Then use affirmations that apply to you.)

NOON

- Have I gone to alpha at least once this morning?
- Have I taken action or made plans to take action on overcoming my fears?
- Have I monitored my thoughts and replaced negative ones with affirmations about myself?
(Then go to alpha and use affirmations and visualizations for reprogramming.)

EVENING

- How many times have I gone to alpha today?
- What action did I take to overcome my fear?
- Have I monitored my thoughts and replaced negative ones with affirmations about myself?
- Have I written in my journal today?
- Have I given myself "attaboys" and "attagirls" for every attempt I have made to help myself and others?
  (Then affirm that you are a worthy person who deserves to be free of fear. Use other affirmations that apply to you.)

BEFORE AN ANXIETY-PRODUCING EVENT

- Have I prepared for this event by going to alpha and visualizing myself enjoying it, completely free of fear? Have I made use of Emotional Transfusion (Chapter 7)?
- Have I prepared cue cards that I can take with me to remind myself to focus outward?
- Have I considered any negative cognitions I have about this event, and have I replaced them with affirmations?
- Have I affirmed that I deserve to be calm and enjoy this event? Have I affirmed that I love the little child within me who is feeling nervous?

The Two-Month Monitor

For your Two-Month Monitor, ask yourself the following questions, and write your answers in your journal:

- What progress have I made in the past two months?
- Have I rewarded myself for this progress? If not, what treat will I give myself today?
- In what areas have I progressed less than I had hoped?
- What new goals will help me overcome these problems?
- How will I carry out these goals?
- Have I used my progress in any way to help others who have the same problems, such as encouraging them verbally or working in a support group?

By using my Fourteen-Day Plan to implement the FEAR-Smashers and monitoring daily and bimonthly, you will start recovering from anxiety and irrational fears quickly. As you continue to progress, you will learn to refine and polish your goals, affirmations, visualizations, and thoughts until they are much more helpful than the ones with which you started. You will find yourself risking new activities, friends, careers, and hobbies. You will find that it is an exciting adventure to be recovering from your fears!

PART

II

THE FEAR-SMASHER KEYS

5

MAKING THE COMMITMENT TO CHANGE: THE FIRST FEAR-SMASHER KEY

O NE DAY a psychologist who has worked with many
fearful people came to see me.

"Bob, I've read your book, and it seems to me that
you use a lot of the same cognitive restructuring that I teach
my clients. But not everybody I try to help gets over fear. Is
there anything else you did that you could tell me about?"

I began to think about that. It seemed to me I had written
everything I knew about getting over fears in *Anxiety and
Panic Attacks*. Still, what he said rang a bell. In fact, the
ringing of my telephone at midnight a few days earlier had
made me realize that simply knowing *how* to recover is not
the same thing as actually recovering. I told him about the
incredible phone conversation I had had that night. A housebound agoraphobic, her voice trembling with excitement,
related that she had read a few chapters of the book and now
believed she could get well. Then she asked if I had any other
printed material I could send her.

"I couldn't believe it. She hadn't even finished the book and
she was asking for more information," I said. "I told her she
needed to read the book through two or three times if necessary. She needed to commit herself to taking responsibility
for her own wellness. Then she needed to practice the Five

Basic Principles over and over in her own life for a few months, at least."

We both agreed that fear is like any habit. You can get over a habit if you become aware that you have it and then make a commitment to practice the simple actions like my FEAR-Smashers that will enable you to change. If you don't make that commitment, and if you keep telling yourself that you're a victim, you won't recover. When you tell yourself that you're a victim, you give away the responsibility for your wellness to your parents, therapists, doctors, pills, drugs, or anything else outside yourself that you can blame. You never make use of the fear-breaking tools, so your fear habit stays with you.

"That's true, Bob. But a lot of people aren't self-starters. How did you make yourself practice the Five Basic Principles?" the psychologist asked.

"I made a commitment to do *whatever it took* to get over my agoraphobia. I put it all down in writing. But wait a minute. Maybe I can show you," I said. I went into the bathroom, opened a drawer, and rummaged around in it. Far in the back I found the crumpled, yellowing piece of paper I had written on six years before. I brought it to the psychologist.

"Take a look at this," I said. He read it out loud:

"1. I will be cheerful.
"2. I will use my unconscious to build my feelings of self-worth.
"3. I will smile three times a day.
"4. I will be friendly to three people each day."

While the psychologist was reading my old goal sheet, I realized that I had become everything I had wanted to be. I *was* friendly, cheerful, assured of my self-worth, and able to value others.

The psychologist, however, didn't seem too impressed with my goal sheet.

"Is that all you did?" he asked.

"That's not the half of it," I told him. "I did more than just look at those goals every morning. I made a point of practicing them every day. And before I went to bed at night I checked off whether or not I had done each one."

"Sounds as if you thought that committing yourself to achieving your goals was pretty important," he said.

"It was. I knew that if I didn't, I wasn't ever going to be free of those awful panic attacks. I was going to continue to be a negative, frightened, insecure person, whom I didn't like very much."

The First FEAR-Smasher Key: First, Make a Commitment

I have placed this FEAR-Smasher key first because it is the most important of all. Without it, you can't get over your fear.

> The First FEAR-Smasher Key: *First,* make a commitment to overcome your fear habit; then take responsibility for understanding your fear and changing your attitude toward it.

Webster's defines *commitment* as "an agreement or pledge to do something in the future." I'm convinced that if you want to get over the fear habit, you have to do more than just pledge. First, you have to recognize that you are afraid and define what you are afraid of. Then you must take responsibility for acting to overcome this fear.

Sometimes it's hard to admit that we are fearful. I've heard people say that their heart pounds so hard and their mouth gets so dry every time they have to drive, go to a shopping center, or attend a social function that they'll do almost anything to avoid doing those things. Yet they won't admit to their spouses that they really are afraid. Why? "He might think I was going crazy." "She wouldn't love me anymore," they say.

Other people tell me that they just feel uncomfortable doing things that everyone else seems to enjoy—like being on a crowded beach, at a concert, at an art museum, or at a party. They feel so uncomfortable that they refuse invitations to go. "That's just the way I am," they tell themselves, with a wistful look in their eyes.

Sometimes we don't even realize that we are afraid. Suppose we gain recognition for meeting a sales quota, advancing in our work, or cooking a wonderful dinner for friends. Then we sabotage our success by performing badly on the next important task. It seems almost as if we do it deliberately, and so we do, if we fear success. But we may never recognize that that kind of fear has us in its grip.

If you want to stop being afraid, you have to commit youself to five actions:

1. Admitting that you have a specific fear
2. Taking responsibility for acting in ways that will enable you to break the fear habit
3. Learning all you can about what causes that kind of fear
4. Setting goals for turning your fears into assets
5. Working on the goals every day

From Victim to Victor

Owning up to your fears may be painful, but it has a payoff in the form of *power for recovering.* I can't help but think about Debbie, who told me that she had "gone through hell" thirteen years earlier when her phobia about driving turned into a series of panic attacks. After four years of misery, Debbie fought back. She made the commitment to get well, and she desensitized herself to her phobias with very little help from others. She made herself go places. When she thought she would faint or make a complete fool of herself, she just kept on going. Eventually the panic attacks went away completely—or so she thought. Nine peaceful years later, Debbie's body reacted to the stress of losing her job and having marital problems. Out of the blue, she had another panic attack. But by this time she had found my Five Basic Principles. She had better tools to work with.

"I don't have to be a 'victim' of panic attacks," she wrote me. "From reading your book, I have discovered that it is up to me to change my attitude. I am the only one who can do something about the panic attacks."

The Responsibility Quiz

Answer the following questions to determine whether or not you are taking the responsibility for your fear:

1. When fears prevent me from doing things that other people consider normal or fun, do I make up excuses that I know aren't true?
2. Do I tend to blame my childhood for not being able to do what I want as an adult?
3. Do I say that my spouse, my children, my in-laws, or my friends stand in the way of my doing anything about my fear?
4. Have I refused to tell my spouse or other important persons in my life about my fears?
5. Is my excuse for being afraid that "I just can't help it"?
6. Do I put off doing anything about my fear because I'm waiting for a miracle drug that will cure me?
7. Have I tried to work on my fears but have given up?

If you answered yes to several of these questions, there is a strong possibility that you are playing the victim. This quiz is not intended to make you feel guilty. I have included it here to help you make a commitment to stop playing life-limiting games. Be good to yourself. Claim the power that you will receive by making a commitment to get well. It's not so hard, and the reason it isn't is that you can use goal-setting and goal-working to make it easier.

The "Goal" Way to Recovery

As a criminal attorney, Richard "Racehorse" Haynes has won international fame for successfully defending prestigious clients. *Blood Will Tell* recounts his defense of millionaire Cullen Davis, accused of killing two people and wounding another in his Fort Worth mansion. The best-seller *Blood and Money* tells how he convinced a jury that Houston doctor

John Hill did not kill his wife. Yet Haynes related in a profile in the *Dallas Morning News* on August 3, 1986, that the first time he went to court, he was so nervous that he tripped over a spittoon in front of the jury box. The jurors laughed.

If Haynes had been like most fearful people, this incident alone might have been embarrassing and stressful enough to cause him to develop a phobia of courtrooms. But Haynes seems to be a naturally positive person, someone who wakes up every day believing that good things happen to him because he deserves them. "I have good thoughts in my heart. When you have good thoughts in your heart, good things happen to you," he was reported as saying.

The article told how Haynes went on to win that case, not only because he was prepared to defend his client but also because his mishap had helped him make a bond with the jurors. After that, "Racehorse" made sure that he stumbled over it every time he went to court.

We aren't all blessed with Haynes's natural philosophy of positive thinking, but we can develop it. (Chapter 6 will show you how to do that.) Yet once we admit our fears, we can use the FEAR-Smasher keys the way Haynes used the spittoon: as tools to help us become winners. We can make sure that we use the tools by setting goals.

How to Write Your Goals

For each fear that you have, you should make a goal sheet in your notebook. You will also want to have a general goal sheet to improve your self-esteem, because a good self-image is the most effective way of overcoming fears.

Here are nine tips for writing your goals and making it easy to work on them:

1. Once you have identified your long-term goals, subdivide them into a series of short-term goals. Breaking long-term goals down into easy-to-do, bite-sized actions makes them seem less insurmountable. Here is how some goal sheets would look for a person who has a fear of heights:

Long-Term Goal: I will overcome my fear of heights.

Short-Term Goals:

1. I will go to alpha three times a day and visualize and affirm myself as being entirely free of fear when I am in high places.
2. I will work on desensitization so that I can gradually go closer to tall buildings, then enter them, and, finally, ride the elevator to the top.
3. I will act *as if* I am free of fear.

2. Each of the short-term goals should be on a separate sheet. Now divide these into subgoals, using tips from the five FEAR-Smasher keys. Be sure to leave space for a daily checkoff list, so you can keep track whether you worked on each of the subgoals each day. Head this checklist "Attaboys" or "Attagirls," and designate the days of the week beneath this heading.

Here is how the third short-term goal in point 2 might look when broken down into subgoals with an attaboy/attagirl checklist:

3. I will act *as if* I am free of fear.

Subgoals	*Attagirls*
	S M T W T F S

• I will smile when I am walking past tall buildings.

• I will tell other people that I have learned some new tools that will enable me to be free of my fear.

• I will write in my journal about the successes I am having in approaching tall buildings.

3. Be specific in describing the ways in which you plan to use the FEAR-Smasher keys. (You'll learn more about the keys and how to write goals based on them in the next four chapters.)

4. Prioritize your goals. Although you should write lots of goal sheets, choose no more than three to concentrate on daily.

5. Give yourself plenty of time to achieve your goals. Remember that you are learning skills, and the way you learn to get over fears is just the way you learn to play golf or tennis or to swim. You don't go out the first day and hit your golf ball with just the right form. It takes time. You will need to practice your goals over and over for days before the change in your unconscious will come about, freeing you from your fear. How long is long enough? Each individual will have a different timetable, but for most of us, a few months suffice. Just hold on to the thought that every day that you practice your goals, they become easier to do the next day. Eventually you won't even have to think about them. They will be a part of your unconscious.

6. Make a morning ritual of reading your goals. Most of us do have a ritual every morning for making ourselves clean and good-looking on the outside. We just need to go one step farther and make a commitment to make ourselves clean, good-looking, and *calm* on the inside, too. I found my old goal sheet in the bathroom drawer because I made a point of reading my goal sheet every morning, between showering and brushing my teeth. Reading the goal sheet simply became one more part of my morning ritual.

7. Reinforce your goals. Every morning when I looked at my goal sheet, I repeated the goals *aloud*. I told myself that I was a worthy person. I deserved to be committed to my goals.

8. Every evening before you go to bed, check whether you have worked the goals. (Once again, toothbrushing time

can be a reminder to include the checklist as a part of your evening grooming ritual.) Read the goals and ask yourself these questions:

- Did I smile when I had to walk past that tall building on the way to work this morning? This evening?
- How many people did I tell that I now had the tools to overcome my feelings of fear?

Then give yourself an "attaboy" or an "attagirl" check for each time you did something positive to get over your fear.

9. Write down the positive things you did other than working the goals in your daily journal. Forget all the failures, the what-if's, the anger you feel about not having accomplished more than you did. In other words, try hard to find something positive you did that day, and then give yourself lots of good strokes for having done it.

The Learning Goal

Through my lectures for the Phobia Centers of the Southwest, I have become acquainted with Bill Evans, the American Airlines pilot who has helped psychologists Jim Wilson and Robert Ingram teach many people how to get over their fear of flying. The psychologists teach the fear-stopping tools. Bill's job is to teach clients all about flying: aerodynamics, why a plane cannot simply fall out of the sky, what all the mysterious noises are, and the many fine instruments pilots use to overcome bad weather conditions.

Most people who are afraid of flying admit that their real fear is not that the plane will crash. They are afraid that they themselves will go out of control and make a fool of themselves because their irrational fear symptoms are so overpowering. Why, then, should Bill Evans teach them the complexities of aerodynamics and answer questions that range from "What if the turbulence gets too bad and I'm thrown up against the ceiling?" to "What if the engines all stop working?"

The reason is that strange noises and sudden movements on the plane can trigger or exacerbate irrational fears. Anyone who is dealing with fear needs to learn everything possible about the feared situation to be able to confront irrational fears with the cold, hard facts. Education is one way of putting an end to the "what if" thinking that leads to the fear of making a fool of yourself.

So take advantage of every book, course, and article you can find that provides the facts about the thing you fear. When you replace the what-if's with the what-is's, you will be better able to relax and use the FEAR-Smasher keys. You can be more successful at working your goals.

What's in the Future?

By now you can see that I believe goals to be essential for recovering from panic and anxiety. Spend time now writing your goals; then read on and learn to work the other FEAR-Smasher keys. If you do this, someday you too will rediscover your old goal sheets and rejoice that you have become the person you wanted to be.

6

CALLING MR. POSITIVE

BRETT DAVIS, chairman of the board of Troy Nichols, Inc., and Stockton Savings, faced a frightening situation early in his business career. When he was only 22 years old, the real estate investment company he headed had 8000 apartment units in Dallas among its extensive holdings. One day Davis received telephone calls from the utility companies, telling him that they had red-tagged all the Dallas apartments. Because bills hadn't been paid for months, they were threatening to cut off the gas and electricity. Davis knew that without utilities, his tenants would leave by the thousands. He wouldn't be able to save the company from bankruptcy. Coincidentally, he also discovered that an executive of the management company was missing, and so was $8 million in rental collections.

"Yes, I was really frightened, but I didn't take time to think about it," Davis told me. Instead he took action and persuaded bankers to give him a loan. Then he worked day and night for two years to pull the business out of the red. In 1987 the Association of Collegiate Entrepreneurs named him the number one entrepreneur in the country under 30 years of age; his company generated more business than any other company headed by such a young entrepreneur.

His positive attitude also won for him in 1986 the first silver medal ever presented by the prestigious Napoleon Hill Foundation. He was honored as an embodiment of Hill's famous statement, "Whatever the mind can conceive and believe, it can achieve."

In accepting the medal, Davis said, "In the real estate business, you always hear that the three keys are location, location, location. But for success, I would say they are attitude, attitude, attitude."

Then he went on to say something that I believe has a lot of impact for anyone who is afraid. "Anyone can have a positive attitude while everything is going right. It's your attitude about adversity and how you overcome it that determines whether you're really successful or not."

I heartily agree. In *Anxiety and Panic Attacks*, I explained how a negative attitude about irrational fears only increases the power of the fear. "I'm nothing but a failure," you say, giving yourself a reason for avoiding everything you fear. When you do that, you are listening to "Mr. Negative," who only reinforces your poor self-image. I know how this works because I used to do it myself!

My Third Basic Principle showed how to use cognitive restructuring to replace negative thoughts with positive ones. This was a simple way of training the unconscious to give you good feelings about yourself. I explained that when Mr. Negative called to reinforce your thoughts about being unworthy, a fraud, or a second-rate person, you didn't have to answer the phone. You could just let it ring and never pick it up. Mr Negative would get tired of calling and would finally leave you alone.

This strategy works because *negative thinking is nothing more than a bad habit*. You can break that habit by reconditioning yourself to think positively. First, you discover *when* you are thinking negatively by placing blue stickers around your house or office as reminders to ask yourself what you are thinking whenever you see one of them. Another tool you can use is to wear a rubber band on your wrist and snap it every time you discover a negative thought. The little jolt is the signal to replace these negative thoughts with positive ones. The goal is for you to increase your self-esteem by internalizing a positive self-image and a positive attitude toward events in your life.

Now, with my second FEAR-Smasher key, I want you to go one step farther. I want you not only to avoid Mr. Negative; I want you to *call in Mr. Positive.*

The Second FEAR-Smasher Key: *Establish* your self-worth.

The "Self" Words and What They Can Do for You

My second FEAR-Smasher key means going to the phone, dialing Mr. Positive's number, listening to his nurturing statements, and agreeing that they are true! It means living as if they are true already. Once you have Mr. Positive on your side, he will send you self-worth to obliterate outdated childhood images that can cause you to feel guilty or afraid. Mr. Positive can give you Brett Davis's winning attitude.

You *must* have self-worth in order to get over fears. Without it, it is all too easy just to give up and play the victim when life gets rough, With it, you *feel* like going for what you want. Your unconscious, bolstered with good feelings about yourself, helps you put the FEAR-Smasher keys into action. Then it is easy to change your habit of feeling afraid to one of acting positively despite your fear.

I have found that self-worth is made up of four qualities that are described by words that begin with *self.* These words—*self-confidence, self-esteem, self-image,* and *self-love*—are bandied about and frequently misused. Right now I want to clarify their meanings as I define them.

Self-confidence is "confidence in oneself and in one's abilities." As I see it, self-confidence is the feeling of competence and OK-ness you get when you have achieved some successes. This great feeling enables you to venture forth to try to accomplish other great things. You *earn* self-confidence by paying your dues. For instance, you may make such a good business presentation that you win compliments and maybe even a promotion. Then you're ready to excel at a higher level. Or you take a course in home decorating and create a whole new color scheme for your living room that looks so charming that you're inspired to give a party. Or, if you're agoraphobic, you venture out of the house and give yourself an "attaboy" or "attagirl" for doing a great thing—and then go a block farther the next day. Self-confidence is feeling so wonderful about your accomplishments that you are excited and eager to set higher goals and work on them.

Self-esteem, although it sounds the same as self-confidence, is something entirely different. Self-esteem is the inherent value and worth with which you were born. You don't earn self-esteem. It is a gift that is given to you, and no one *but you yourself* can take it away. When you recognize your self-esteem, you are motivated to accomplish great things not because of your past successes but simply because you feel in your bones that you are a worthy human being and you deserve great things. When you have *good* self-esteem, you can't have irrational fears. If you have *poor* self-esteem, however, you *refuse to recognize* that you were born with value and worth. Poor self-esteem leads to feelings that the world, other people, and circumstances are all a threat. These feelings can lead to problems with irrational fears.

Self-image is your conception of yourself or your role. A good self-image enhances self-esteem. A poor self-image destroys self-esteem. Our perceptions of who we are stem largely from our childhood and from the way we, at a very tender age, interpreted the important things that happened to us. As children, however, we lacked the maturity to interpret many events correctly, so our perceptions, or *cognitions* (as psychologists call them), were faulty. Yet as adults, our unconscious sends us feelings based on these mistaken perceptions. If our childhood view of ourselves was that we were bad, frightened, angry, or depressed, then as adults we tend to believe that we're still that way. And we act accordingly.

A friend whom I'll call Sarah was delighted that she was

recovering from having panic attacks. Everything seemed to be going her way, because she had a close relationship with a man whom she fully expected to marry. Then one day her boyfriend told her that he admired her as a friend but that he saw nothing else in their relationship.

Sarah reacted with anger. She told the man whom she had been hoping to marry that he was a selfish, egotistical person who would never amount to anything. She put him down in every way she could.

Even though I understood the rejection Sarah was feeling, I hated to see her react to this painful situation with bitterness. I knew that Sarah's negative attitude wasn't going to help her recover from the loss of what she had thought was love. It would only hurt her and make it more difficult for her to open up to someone else. Furthermore, the stress that built inside her as a result of her resentment caused her panic attacks to resurface. Why was she doing the very thing that would cause herself harm?

I didn't have to think very long. Sarah had had a miserable childhood in which she felt unloved and put down. Although Sarah was now a talented and charming person, she still perceived herself as that little, frightened child overwhelmed with the fear that she wasn't worthy of anyone's love. But Sarah didn't dare let anyone else know about her poor self-image. She was afraid that if she did, they might ridicule her just as others had done when she was a child. Then she would feel worse. She believed that the only thing to do was to go on the offensive and make others feel just as badly as she felt about herself. She hurled accusations at her ex-boyfriend to try to make him feel guilty, but in doing so she only increased the feeling of shame she had about herself.

If you are like Sarah, you let faulty childhood perceptions (a poor self-image) rule the way you will react. You see yourself as a failure in life. You attribute any successes you have to luck or to other outside circumstances. Thus you destroy any possibility of developing self-confidence. That's the bad news. The good news is that you can change your self-image through cognitive restructuring and by calling in Mr. Positive.

Self-love is regard for one's own happiness or progress. It is the commitment to be good to yourself, so that you can change your negative self-image, recognize your unconditional self-esteem, and create successes that will lead to self-confidence. Self-love is believing in Mr. Positive and allowing him to help you eliminate irrational and rational fears.

Let Mr. Positive build your self-confidence, self-esteem, self-image, and self-love, and you will have self-worth, the quality that will allow you to confront any fear and overcome it.

The Self-worth Quiz

In *Anxiety and Panic Attacks*, I taught you the "big ten" of faulty cognitions that diminish your self-worth. I also taught you how to replace them with positive cognitions. Take a few minutes to answer the questions that follow to see whether you have some faulty cognitions that stand in the way of increasing your self-confidence, recognizing your self-esteem, enhancing your self-image, and developing your self-love.

> *1. Am I afraid that because of my divorce, I just don't have what it takes to attract a Mr./Ms. Right the second time around?*

If so, your faulty cognition is *perfectionism*, and it causes you to set unreasonably high standards for yourself and others. Your self-worth is wounded, because you perceive anything less than a perfect relationship as romantic failure. I know from experience how hard it is not to think this way, but if you restructure that faulty cognition, you can overcome the temptation to sabotage yourself in love. Call in Mr. Positive, practice self-love, and recognize that no human being does everything perfectly. We just don't function that way. You are a person of worth regardless of an imperfect relationship. You deserve love, happiness, and self-acceptance as you are. You will then have less anxiety about attracting Mr. or Ms. Right. Chances are, that person will then gravitate toward you, attracted by all that positive energy you are exuding.

2. *Do I work in a "loner" kind of job because I like it or because I just can't stand making errors in front of other people and being corrected in my work?*

If you are trying to escape from what you see as constant criticism, you may be suffering from *rejectionitis*. You perceive your co-workers' minor criticisms of your work as rejection of you as a person. Call in Mr. Positive, and in the spirit of self-love, see criticisms as attempts to help you develop yourself. Change the cognition "They are putting me down because they don't like me" to "They are trying to help me do a better job, and I deserve their help."

3. *Am I avoiding going to places I would like to go for my own enjoyment (such as church, a small social gathering, or the movies) because I am afraid I will suddenly have a panic attack and have to leave?*

If you answered yes, you are using *negative focus* to destroy opportunities for increasing your ability to feel self-esteem. You are telling yourself that everyone will think you are peculiar if you have to leave. Call in Mr. Positive: Replace this faulty cognition with "I am a person of worth who deserves to have a good time with other people. I can explain ahead of time that I have had panic attacks in the past. If I have to leave they will understand, just as I would understand if other people had a physical condition that caused them to leave."

4. *Am I concentrating on how far I have to go before I am over my fears and ignoring the progress I have already made?*

If so, you are *refusing the positives*. You are telling yourself that even the good things in your life, the small accomplishments that lead to self-confidence and the ability to keep trying, are negatives. Call in Mr. Positive. If you have to use a mental microscope to see anything good about what you are doing, then do it! Tell yourself, "Today I worked on my goals, and I accomplished one of them. That's wonderful." It really is!

5. *Am I asking a lot of "what if" questions that increase my anxiety?*

If so, you are thinking in *white-is-black* terms. You are making faulty predictions that everything you do will have dire consequences. For instance, if you're afraid to make a speech, you may spend the time while you're being introduced asking yourself, "What if my voice starts shaking so that I can't talk? What if my mind goes blank? What if I make a complete fool of myself?" When you do white-is-black thinking, you only increase your anxiety, and your body fulfills your expectations by sending you fear sensations. Call in Mr. Positive and replace *what if* with *so what if?* "So what if my voice shakes, my mind goes blank, and the speech is less successful than I want? Even a poor performance does not diminish the fact that I am a worthy person, born with as much value as everyone else."

6. *Am I telling myself that even though I haven't had a panic attack for a long time now, I'm bound to have one because everyone says a relapse is inevitable? Am I telling myself that I'm less than a success because, after all, panic attacks did dominate my life for years?*

If so, you are doing *stretch-or-shrink thinking.* You are *stretching* the truth by saying you're bound to relapse, and you are also destroying self-confidence, self-esteem, and self-worth. At the same time you are *shrinking* the value of all the hard work you have already done to rid yourself of panic attacks. Mr. Positive can reverse stretch-or-shrink thinking. You can *diminish* your fears about a relapse by telling yourself, "Many people, like Bob Handly, have been free of panic attacks for years. I am not likely to relapse, because I have used the same methods he uses. If I do, it's no big deal, because I have the tools to stop them again, and I know I have done it once successfully." You can *inflate* rather than shrink the value of the work you have done by giving yourself lots of "attaboys" or "attagirls."

7. *Am I telling myself it's all right for other people to work on desensitizing themselves to their phobias, but as for me, I'm just paralyzed by fear?*

If so, you are creating *fictional fantasies*. You are letting your fear create a harmful fantasy about yourself, and your unconscious is accepting your fantasy and reinforcing it with the lie that it is impossible for you to help yourself. Call in Mr. Positive and see the reality about yourself. Just because you *feel* fear does not mean that you have to give in to it. Accept the fact that you have feelings of fear; then *nurture your self-image* by telling yourself how much you love yourself. I'll be showing you better ways to do this later on in this chapter.

8. *Am I always telling myself that "I should quit smoking, I ought to lose weight, I should be making more progress than I am?"*

Thinking in *"should" and "ought" legalisms* only causes you to feel guilt. You really don't have to please some imaginary boss. Call in Mr. Positive and realize that *you* are the only one whom you want to please. If you decide that you want to quit smoking or lose weight because you love yourself and you are worth the effort, set long- and short-term goals to do so. Work on your goals gradually, and give yourself lots of positive feedback. Your self-esteem will go up rather than down as you progress.

9. *Am I secretly telling myself that I deserve to have panic attacks because, after all, my kids have problems, and I must have been the one to cause them?*

If so, you are practicing *"My fault!"* thinking. You are assuming responsibility for your children's failures even when the responsibility is not yours. If your children fail courses, abuse drugs, or vandalize your neighbor's home, you don't have to assume all the blame. Your children have the responsibility to do their homework and to say no to peer pressure. Crying "My fault!" only increases your anxiety. It does nothing for your children, because you can't do for them what they must do for themselves. In fact, it would be bad for them if you tried to make their decisions for them. Call in Mr. Positive by affirming that you are giving your children all the love you have and that it is up to them to do with their lives whatever they will. Freed from guilt, you will actually be better able to focus on their needs and find the proper help for their problems.

10. Do I tell myself that I'm all bad because I had an affair that caused my spouse a lot of pain?

If so, your faulty cognition is *mistaken identity.* You don't have to take a baseball bat and hit yourself over the head every day because you made a mistake. The reality of life is that everybody makes mistakes. Don't dwell on what you did; dwell on what you *learned.* Then call in Mr. Positive, forgive yourself, and set goals to relate lovingly to your spouse. Use mistakes as tools for learning, and your self-esteem will go up rather than down.

Increasing Your Perception of Worthiness

Now that you have reviewed the "big ten" of faulty cognitions, you may be thinking, "Yes, I can see that I have been thinking negatively about some things and I want to restructure my faulty cognitions. But at the time I am thinking in faulty cognitions, I'm not very rational. My emotions get in the way."

If you are unable to challenge faulty cognitions, the reason may be that you are settling for less than your fair share of worthiness feelings. It's as if you had a thermometer that measures positive feelings. For everyone else, you know that 98.6 degrees is normal. For yourself, you see normal as 80 or even lower. Because of a poor self-image, you may unconsciously believe that your thermometer *should* register your normal worthiness lower than everyone else's. And you may act accordingly.

Gina's worthiness rating was very low because she had an alcoholic father who had made her a scapegoat as a child. As an adult, phobias and anxiety prevented her from having fun with other people. She didn't like being phobic, but unconsciously she thought of herself as someone who was walking under a rain cloud. If anything bad happened, it was *her fault;* try as hard as she could, she was bound to fail *(stretch-or-shrink thinking).* She often felt that she *should* do something to improve, but what was the use?

Gina needed to reduce the guilt she felt by refusing to use the words *should* and *ought.* She needed to stop blaming herself for things that went wrong that really weren't her fault. And instead of telling herself that she was a bad person when she made mistakes, she needed to be able to say, "I made a mistake, but that's OK."

At first Gina's worthiness rating was too low for her even to believe that she could restructure her faulty cognitions. Then she learned how to increase her perception of worthiness (as I'll show you how to do in a moment). She found that she could nurture herself, and then she slowly came to believe that she deserved success in changing her thoughts about herself. When she made this discovery, Gina was able to restructure her cognitions.

Nurturing the Little Child Within You

Psychologists tell us that deep inside of us lives the little child we were when we were 4 or 5 years old. In childhood, we took in all the negative comments made by parents, other kids, teachers, and even strangers, and we decided then and there that that was all we were worth.

If Mother was angry because your room looked as if a tornado had hit it and she declared, "You're a lazy girl," your unconscious took in the fact that you were lazy. If your big brother teased, "You're nothing but a nerd," you added that perception of yourself. When you didn't do your homework and your teacher complained, "You'll never amount to a thing," you decided that she was right. And when the little boy you had a crush on told you your freckles were ugly, your unconscious added ugliness to your poor self-image. How could you possibly deserve anything good in life?

When you consider all the negative input you received (even if those who gave it to you didn't really mean it), you can understand why you might feel that you don't deserve success in work, in love, or in freedom from phobias and fears. You may even decide that the thing you *ought* to do is to continue to criticize this little child that lives within you. "No wonder good things never happen to you," you tell yourself, as you repeat what your mother, brother, teacher, and boyfriend said. "You just don't deserve them."

This self-criticism increases your depression, your feelings of incompetence, and your dislike of your body, your personality, and your achievements. It sets your worthiness rating low, and it drains you of energy for making improvements.

No matter how bad your childhood was, however, you can raise your perception of your worthiness. Instead of criticizing your little child, you can make a commitment to *nurture* him or her. You can be the enlightened parent, the loyal sibling, the inspiring teacher, or the loving friend who accepts you as you are and builds you up with good, kind affirmations.

Let's look at the difference between self-criticism and self-nurturing. Suppose that you are afraid to drive a car. You've had to ask your husband one more time to leave work to take the children to the doctor, and he has reacted with an angry "You could drive if you really wanted to. Why don't you just do it?" Rage and resentment overcome you. You want to hit him, cry, and feel sorry for yourself. At the same time, guilt nags at you. "There must be something wrong with me. After all, everyone else I know can drive."

If you give in to the self-criticism that most of us use, you tell your little angry 5-year-old internal child, "You're a failure. You should be able to drive, and it's all your fault that your husband is mad. You'll never be able to do any better. You might as well give up." Your little child feels blamed and reacts with further anger and more depression.

If you have pledged to nurture yourself, however, you will stand back, remind yourself that you are feeling angry and resentful, and assert that *now is the time to be a friend to yourself.* Consider how you (the loving parent) would nurture yourself (the angry, resentful child). You might say, "I know you are feeling angry and resentful. It's OK. Everyone feels that way sometimes. You have many good qualities. You are a generous, caring person. I love you." Your little child then accepts her angry feelings and is reassured that she is still loved. She begins to believe that she is *worth* the effort of working on a goal of being able to drive. As your improved self-image helps you accomplish little successes that are further nurtured with "attagirls," you develop more self-confidence. Your little successes lead to more and larger triumphs. Before long you are able to overcome your phobias.

You can use self-nurturing techniques to overcome the bad effects of any emotions that are destroying your self-worth.

The Spiritual Connection

One other thing you can do to increase your self-worth is to realize that everything you are is a gift from your creator. Remember that you were born with inherent worth. If you have lost touch with it, bring in the aid of the creator who gave it to you in the first place. You can accomplish this with meditation, prayer, religion—any way that seems best to you to connect with the spiritual part of your being.

If you make a goal to get more in touch with your spiritual self, you may find that it is easier to do cognitive restructuring. Your spiritual self, which loves and nurtures you automatically, will build your self-esteem. In a later chapter I will explain more about the important role the spiritual connection plays in combating fear and anxiety.

Getting Started

Cognitive restructuring doesn't just happen. Here are some things you can write about in your notebook under the second FEAR-Smasher key to help you get started:

- In one column, write down as many negative statements as you can remember about your childhood. Use the "big ten" list of negative cognitions to determine exactly how you are thinking. In another column, counter each negative cognition with a rational, positive cognition.
- Set a goal to nurture yourself. Write down the words you will use whenever you need to overcome some of the feelings you experience about the negative statements you heard as a child.

Underneath your stated goal of self-nurturance, make two columns. Under the "Negative Cognition" heading, write what someone said or did to you as a child that made you feel bad about yourself. In the "Positive Nurturing Statements" column, write the nurturing thoughts that you will use to neutralize them.

Your notebook might look something like this:

Goal: I want to increase my perception of my worthiness by restructuring the negative thoughts that resulted when my older brother said that I was stupid.

Negative Cognition	Positive Nurturing Statements
I am stupid. It's all my fault that I can't overcome my phobia about driving.	You are feeling angry and resentful because you have been called stupid. That's OK. You

are pretty
smart about a
lot of things,
especially the
way you can do
the income tax,
cook, sew, and
take care of the
children. I love
you.

Whenever you are feeling strong emotions and Mr. Negative has you in his grip, take out your notebook and read the nurturing statements you have written about yourself. Then nurture yourself by repeating them out loud. Eventually you will have mastered the second FEAR-Smasher key. You will automatically believe that you deserve good things, and you will be able to counter faulty cognitions quickly without the use of the notebook.

7

THE PHYSICAL CONNECTION

D R WILLIAM KEMP CLARK, professor and chairman of neurology at the University of Texas Southwestern Medical School at Dallas, is a man who has profound respect for the human brain. In 1986 some of the world's most prominent neurosurgeons gathered in Dallas to honor him for his part in shaping the training programs and direction of neurosurgery in the United States.

During a break in the meeting, Clark told a *Dallas Morning News* reporter, "It is just awesome to think of what it [the brain] does. . . . You have an organ that doesn't make any noise, it doesn't move and there's no pain there. And yet it can do all this," he said, waving his hand at the magnificent atrium of the Loews Anatole Hotel where he sat.

In the *Dallas Morning News*, Dr. Clark was quoted as saying that he uses his own brain in a way that seems even more impressive to me. The night before he is to perform neurosurgery, he visualizes each intricate step of the operation, including all the contingencies. He believes that this imaginary enactment of the operation will enable his hands to do with greater accuracy what his mind wants when the real surgery begins.

Dr. Clark is not alone in believing that visualizing enhances performance. Sports figures, dancers, musicians, business executives, public speakers, high-wire walkers, teachers—an endless list of people use visualizations as a mental tool to sharpen their physical skills.

Many people who are subject to irrational fears and anxiety have learned this secret, too. Visualization is a powerful tool for convincing your boss—your unconscious mind—to work *for* you rather than *against* you in canceling out the body responses that bring on fear. If you also affirm that you are enjoying doing the things you are visualizing and that you are perfectly calm, you double the effectiveness of this tool.

Alpha-Programming Your Boss to Help You

Both visualizations and affirmations work best if you are in the relaxed state I call alpha. My third FEAR-Smasher key is designed to refine and improve the method of using alpha that I explained in *Anxiety and Panic Attacks*.

The Third FEAR-Smasher Key: *Alpha-program* yourself to be free of fear and deserving of self-worth.

Programming yourself means *making friends with your unconscious* so that it will help rather than hinder you. I call the unconscious "the boss no one told you about" because most of us are unaware of when it is at work, yet it controls us. We may tell ourselves consciously over and over again that we don't want to be afraid, but our unconscious doesn't seem to hear. In this conflict between the unconscious and the conscious mind, the unconscious always wins, hands down. Why? Because *your unconscious takes its directions from your feelings, not your rational thoughts.* Then it feeds them back to you to make you act in a way that may be just the opposite of what you really want.

To see how this works, let's examine the fear of flying. Suppose a very turbulent flight frightened you the last time you had to fly. When the plane began making unfamiliar noises and movements, you felt your stomach knot up, your mouth go dry, and your hands become sweaty. These feelings informed your unconscious, "You are afraid to fly." The next time you bought a ticket, you told yourself, "There is nothing to fear. I have flown many times and not been afriad. I am going to feel fine." But when you boarded the plane, your unconscious "boss" sent you the same butterflies, dry mouth, and sweaty palms.

In order to use the third FEAR-Smasher key to combat your subconscious sabotage, you must first learn to reach the alpha state. You do this by lowering the rate at which your brain is cycling from the active, or beta state (14 or more cycles per second) to the quiet and intuitive alpha state (7–14 cps). At this creative level of the mind, you not only free your body from the braced and tension-ridden posture that you assume when you are actively trying to "fight" fear with your conscious mind; you also have access to your unconscious. In the alpha state you can reprogram your "boss" with visualizations and affirmations. You can give your boss your directions, and eventually he will obey by making you feel free of fear and deserving of self-worth. The next time you board a plane, he will keep your stomach, mouth, and hands free of fear symptoms.

In this chapter I will show you improved methods of relaxing so that you can more easily reach the alpha state. I will also explain how you can improve your visualization and affirmation techniques.

Body Therapy: Another Path to Alpha

The Alpha Script that I developed and use has helped countless people to relax their bodies and minds completely in the alpha state. In this state, you feel no different from the times when you are on the point of falling asleep or when you first wake up in the morning. You are able to think deeply and well. Good ideas just seem to float in from your unconscious without effort.

I have received letters, however, from some people who say that they just can't relax by using the script. I now believe that some people who have fears and phobias are simply afraid to let go and relax. They believe that the only way they can be in control of their fear is to be ever-vigilant, to brace themselves, increase the tension, grind their teeth, and meet fear head on. The script is based on progressive muscle relaxation, a process of tightening the muscles and then loosening them, so that you can know the wonderful way release feels. Most of us love that feeling so much that we can't wait to try to duplicate it as often as we can. But if your unconscious is telling you that it is dangerous to loosen up, this process may not work for you.

If you are having trouble relaxing, you may want to prepare for going into alpha by using body therapy, yoga, or special breathing methods.

Relaxing Your Body with Movement

"Some people cannot relax using passive relaxation techniques such as tapes or bio-feedback. They are unable to use their mind to relax; they use their body. They swim, play golf, walk or dance to relax."

These are the words of Michael L. Freedman, Ph.D., a Cleveland psychologist who uses body movement to help people relax. At a Phobia Society of America Workshop, Dr. Freedman explained that "body movement can interrupt tense body habits and help a person reprogram their body to function in a relaxed state."

How does this work? As Dr. Freedman explained, "Our bodies are born relaxed. We develop tensions in our body as a result of fears, loud noises, criticisms and rejections. These body tensions develop into habits that can be seen in tense postures.

"For some people this tension doesn't develop until late teens or early 20's. The first panic attack further cements these tension habits.

"The Body Movements are designed to interrupt tension habits and allow your body to return to its natural relaxed state. These ideas were originally developed by Moshe Feldinkris to help dancers and athletes move more flexibly and efficiently. They are also very effective in helping overcome chronic anxiety."

If you are going to use these movements successfully, you need to follow these ground rules.

1. When doing body movements, turn your attention to your inner self. Notice how your muscles move or don't move and how your muscles change as they relax and let go.

2. If you have trouble noticing the inner sensations, slow down your movement.

3. Breathing is important. People often hold their breath when they are scared or engaged in emotionally risky activities. You may find yourself holding your breath. Breathe naturally and normally as you do these movements.

4. Wear loose-fitting clothing if possible.

5. These movements are designed to interrupt established mind-body patterns. They may seem awkward at first, but you will experience the value of using movements for relaxation after the first session.

6. "No pain and a lot of gain" is Dr. Freedman's motto. If you feel pain or strain, please do less. Although doing less is difficult for people with anxiety, the very act of slowing down, letting go and doing less are important lessons both psychologically and physically.

7. Practice these movements two times each day for 30 days to interrupt the body's habitual tension anticipation and establish an habitual relaxed anticipation.

Relaxing Head and Shoulders

This movement is designed to reduce tension between the head and shoulders. People who carry their tension in their upper torso, shoulders and neck will find this helpful.

1. Stand in an area that gives you plenty of room to swing your arms.

2. Plant your feet and do not move them as you do the next step.

3. Raise your right arm straight in front of you.

4. Keeping the rest of your body stationary, move your right arm and head to the right as far as they will go *without strain*. Notice how far you can go. This benchmark will change as you relax and become more flexible. Now return to your original position.

5. As you again move your arm to the right, allow your head to move to the left. (Remember: no strain, and *breathe*) and bring your head and arm back to center. This may feel strange or awkward, but it works!

6. Repeat the separation of arm and head seven times. Move slowly, rhythmically, and without strain. Now put your arm down and rest, but don't move your feet.

7. To appreciate your changing tension pattern, raise your right arm again, slowly twist your arm and head to the right, and notice how much further you can go beyond the original benchmark.

8. Return to the central position.

9. Repeat, moving the left arm and head to the LEFT. Get your benchmark, return to center, and now move your left arm to the left and your head to the right seven times. After resting (and still without moving your feet), move your left arm and head to the left to appreciate the increased flexibility you have allowed yourself.

10. Notice how you feel when you feel more flexible. Notice that a more flexible body leads to a more flexible mind. Notice that you can make progress relaxing without pain or strain.

Relaxing Your Torso—Part I

This movement is designed for people who carry their tension in their back, stomach, or chest.

1. Lie flat on your back with arms at your side. Note areas of tension, pressure or tightness in your body as you lie on the floor. Don't try to change these tense areas. They will be benchmarks against which to compare progress.

2. Raise both knees while keeping your feet on the floor.

3. Allow your right knee to drift toward the floor as far as it will go without pain or pressure. Then bring it back to center. Remember to breathe naturally.

4. Repeat this movement seven times.

5. Now allow your left leg to drift slowly to the left as far as it will go without pain or pressure, then return to center. Do this seven times.

6. Remember to breathe.

7. Stretch out your legs on the floor and enjoy the changes that are occurring in your body.

Relaxing Your Torso—Part II

The second part of "Relaxing Your Torso" is designed to help you relax even more deeply. Remember to allow your breathing to be natural and keep your attention on your inner sensations as you move.

1. Again, lie on your back, with arms at your side, and notice the tension level of your body. This tension level benchmark will again be helpful in acknowledging your progress toward relaxing.

2. Raise your knees, keeping your feet on the ground.

3. Cross your right leg over your left knee and rest your right leg on your left knee.

4. Now let your left leg drift to the left. Your right leg is carried to your left by your left knee. Then return to center. You'll notice that this movement twists your upper torso (remember: no pain or strain). If you feel pain or strain you are twisting too far.

5. With your right leg still balanced on your left kneecap, allow your left leg to move to the left. Move your head to the right. Move slowly, allowing your torso to feel the twist: if you feel pain or strain, reduce the amount of twist.

6. Repeat Step Five seven times.

7. If you extend your legs on the floor and rest before you repeat this movement for the right leg, you'll notice an interesting change in your body. One side of your body will feel relaxed, heavier and in greater contact with the floor. This will equalize after the next movement.

8. Raise your knees, cross the left leg over the right leg resting your left leg on your right kneecap. Allow your right leg to drift to the right while your head moves to the left. Repeat seven times.

9. Now extend your legs on the floor and enjoy the deepening relaxation that is flooding through your body. Notice how safe and comfortable deep relaxation can feel. Remember your benchmarks of body tension? Have you changed?

10. As you allow your body to discover a more relaxed posture, notice what attitude or thought you need to relax.

Relaxing Your Pelvic Region

Most people with chronic tension will find their pelvic area frozen. Rigidity in the pelvic area is not only uncomfortable, but leads to other body tensions. It is healthy to allow your pelvis and hips total flexibility.

1. Lie on your back and notice any points of pain or pressure.

2. Raise your legs with your feet on the floor.

3. Experiment with rowing your pelvic region toward your face and away from your face.
   When you move your pelvis you'll notice that your back and stomach must also move. When you roll away from your face your back will arch and stomach will protrude, when you roll toward your face your back will bow and stomach repress. You'll also notice that your head follows your pelvis up and down. Allow this to happen.

4. Your legs can help to push your pelvis toward and away from your face. Let your feet and legs do the work of pushing and pulling. With a little practice you'll be able to get this.

5. Repeat this movement as many times as you like so long as you feel comfortable. If you tire or find yourself trying too hard, stop the movement, extend your legs on the floor, and rest. You can then repeat the movement again for as long as you like, so long as you feel comfortable. You'll notice a profound sense of peace and inner harmony following this movement.

If you are the type of person who really benefits from these movements, you can get more information by contacting the Feldinkris Guild, Washington, D.C. 202-723-3030 or Dr. Michael Freedman, Cleveland, Ohio 216-831-3100.

Better Breathing to Reach Alpha

For some people, another hindrance to reaching alpha is not being able to breathe properly. A couple of letters I received show that there are two ways in which many anxious people breathe improperly.

Delores first noticed her breathing problem when she was trying to drive on a bridge one night. "All of a sudden I froze up. I felt as though I couldn't breathe. I was afraid I was going to die," she wrote. After that terrifying night, she began to experience the same symptoms when she had to enter a high-rise building. Her inability to breathe at these times became so bad that one day she ended up in a hospital. A doctor gave her Valium, which didn't help at all.

Delores's breathing problem comes from an archaic defense mechanism that you can still see in animals like rabbits. When hunted, they "freeze," even restricting their breathing in the hope that if they do not move, they won't be seen. When Delores tells herself that she is frightened or threatened, she restricts her breathing. The ensuing lack of oxygen stresses her body chemically, intensifying her fear sensations.

Tina had the opposite problem. One day when she went to a big shopping mall, her heart began to beat rapidly. She started breathing too fast and began to feel dizzy. Tina was hyperventilating: She was breathing so rapidly from her upper chest that she was eliminating too much carbon dioxide from her body. These chemical changes also caused fear symptoms. She, too, ended up in a hospital for her mysterious and frightening breathing problems.

People who tend to be anxious shouldn't wait until they are having a panic attack to train themselves to breathe in the proper way. Many psychologists, like Dr. Christopher McCullough of the San Francisco Phobia Recovery Center, advocate slow, deep breathing as a way of avoiding the chemical overload that creates panic. Such breathing also creates a calm state, one in which it is easier to go into alpha.

Here are some suggestons about breathing:

- Learn to do abdominal breathing—the kind you naturally do when drifting into sleep—and do it *all the time.* Simply breathe in gently and deeply. Place your hand on your abdomen to be sure that as you breathe in, your abdomen pushes out slightly. Exhale slowly and smoothly, focusing on the process to be sure that you breathe out almost all the air in your lungs. If you are exhaling properly, your abdomen will sink in slightly.
- Use the "Calming Counts" technique as taught by Dr. Reid

Wilson of the Clinical Hypnosis Training Program at the Southeast Institute, Chapel Hill, North Carolina. In his book *Don't Panic*, Dr. Wilson says that this way of breathing will help you regain calm when you are feeling anxiety. You can also incorporate it into the process of going to alpha, to help you relax more completely.

There are six steps to the Calming Counts technique:

1. Sit comfortably.
2. Take a long, deep breath and exhale it slowly while saying the word *relax* silently.
3. Close your eyes.
4. Count backward from ten to one while taking ten natural, easy breaths. (On breath one say "ten," on breath two "nine," and so on.)
5. While you are breathing comfortably, notice any tensions, perhaps in your jaw or forehead or stomach. Imagine those tensions loosening.
6. When you reach "one," you may open your eyes, if desired, or keep them closed and proceed with the Alpha Script.

The Alpha Script

Here is the Alpha Script as I used it to learn to reach the alpha state. If you desire, you may add body therapy or Calming Counts to the progressive muscle relaxation that I use. The Alpha Script works best if you tape it, either in your own voice or in someone else's. As you listen, lie down or sit in a relaxed position in a quiet, private room with your eyes closed.

The "secret resting place" mentioned in the script is a pleasant, calming scene that you visualize so intensely that you feel you are actually there. Simply choose the most relaxing place you have ever found, and picture it vividly in your mind. Actually *be* beside that quiet lake on a calm day, or floating on an inner tube in a tranquil pool, or swaying in a childhood swing, or snuggling into your grandmother's feather mattress. Wherever you "are," note all the details of the scene—the colors, the smells, the way your body feels, and the sounds.

Here is the script:

You are feeling very comfortable, very quiet, very calm and peaceful, and soon you will be going into alpha, a normal, creative level of the mind.

Now you will begin to tighten you muscles to the count of four, clenching them as tightly as possible and holding them tensed to the count of four, then releasing them to the count of four. Starting with your head and shoulders, you are now tightening the muscles in your face, jaw, neck, and shoulders. Study the tension. Become aware of what it feels like so you will be able to recognize it when you are awake. One, two, three, four. *(The counting period should last a total of five to seven seconds.)* Hold, two, three, four. Now release these muscles, two, three, four. Tighten, two, three, four; hold, two, three, four; release, two, three, four. Tighten, two, three, four; hold, two, three, four; release, two, three, four. Tighten, two, three, four; hold, two, three, four; release, two, three, four. Become aware of how the relaxation feels as you let go.

You will now tighten the muscles in your hands by making a fist. Tighten, two, three, four; hold, two, three, four; release, two, three, four. *(Repeat four more times.)*

You will now tighten the muscles in your arms, making them as stiff and rigid as you can. Curl your arms up as you would when you flex your arm muscles. Tighten, two, three, four; hold, two, three, four; release, two, three, four. *(Repeat four more times.)*

You will now tighten the muscles in your chest and abdomen. Tighten, two, three, four; hold, two, three, four; release, two, three, four. *(Repeat four more times.)*

You will now tighten the muscles in your pelvis and buttocks area. Tighten, two, three, four; hold, two, three, four; release, two, three, four. *(Repeat four more times.)*

You will now tighten the muscles in your feet and toes. Tighten, two, three, four; hold, two, three, four; release, two, three, four. *(Repeat four more times.)*

You will now tighten the muscles in your legs. Tighten, two, three, four; hold, two, three, four; release, two, three, four. *(Repeat four more times.)*

Always notice what it feels like when you relax your muscles. You are now feeling very calm and rested, in complete control. You are feeling relaxed and fine.

You will now begin to do deep breathing. You will breathe in through your nose and out through your mouth. You will let your stomach rise as you inhale as deeply as possible to the count of four. As you exhale to the count of four you will completely empty the contents of your lungs and let your stomach drop. Your lungs are now filling in the lower part of your abdomen, one; in your chest area, two; up, up, up, three, four. Hold your breath, two, three, four; exhale two, three, four. Each time you breathe in, your body will become heavier and heavier. Again concentrate on letting go all over your body. *(Repeat four more times.)*

Now you will picture your body as being totally relaxed. Imagine that you are like a limp rubber doll, in which the rubber is all stretched out and the stuffing is gone. Imagine that your scalp is becoming loose and tingly. The rubber of your scalp is so loose and pliable that it sags down on your forehead. The skin of your face sags around your eyes. A soft, gentle breeze caresses your face, and it feels very good. Allow your mouth to droop like a rubber mask. Now your jaw has completely dropped and you are releasing all tensions there.

Imagine that your arms are like rubber. They are hanging limply from your shoulders. Your torso is so limp that it hangs on your spine. Your legs are like rubber bands, dangling from your hips. Your feet are detached from your body, connected only by a thread. Imagine that you are floating in a warm, sparkling liquid. You are completely relaxed and in control of your mind and body. You are at a deeper, healthier level of the mind. Yet you are feeling aware and can function exactly as you wish.

To enter a deeper, healthier level of the mind, imagine that you are going down a staircase. With each step down you are becoming more and more relaxed. Count backward from ten to one as you go down the stairs. Ten, nine, eight, seven, six, five, four, three, two, one. You are feeling fine and are using your improved mental faculties to help yourself and others. You are perfectly relaxed, completely calm, and in a moment you will be going to your secret resting place. You will count backward from three to one, and at the count of one you will be in your secret resting place, enjoying the calm, the quiet, the peace, the joy. Three, two, one.

(Allow five minutes of silence at this point.)

You are now completely in control of your thoughts. You are feeling rested and relaxed.

You are now going to count from one to five, and at the count of five, you will open your eyes and be wide awake, feeling fine and in perfect health. You will be feeling better and better. One, two, coming up slowly, slowly; three—at the count of five you will be opening your eyes, wide awake, feeling fine and in perfect health—four, five. Say, "I am wide awake, feeling fine and in perfect health."

More Effective Ways to Visualize

Visualizations and affirmations are the tools that permit you to reprogram yourself while at alpha. A visualization is simply a *controlled daydream* in which you see yourself as if you were a character in a movie, acting the way you want to be, not the way you fear you are. Make use of the five senses to hear, see, feel, smell, and touch whatever is in your movie. The purpose of visualizations is to train your unconscious boss to believe that you are already calm, relaxed, and happy at parties, eating alone, driving on a bridge, making a speech, or doing anything else that brings on fear symptoms.

Affirmations are statements to yourself that you are already the way you want to be. Affirming that you *enjoy* being at parties, eating alone, driving on a bridge, or making a speech further convinces your unconscious to send you good feelings at times when you normally feel nervous. Affirming that you are a worthy person who deserves happiness increases your feelings of self-worth, making it easier for you to confront challenges.

With the growing popularity of *neurolinguistic program-ming*, I see ways to make visualizing and affirming even more effective. I have already explained (in Chapter 3) the basic therapy and how it works to eliminate phobias. Some psychiatrists add a further step when helping their clients dissociate themselves from their phobias. After clients visualize a pleasant experience, the psychiatrist anchors in the calm feelings by touching the right forearm. Next the clients visualize the first time they remember being afraid of a phobic situation. The psychiatrist anchors in the second visualization by touching the client on the opposite forearm. Next clients are asked to visualize themselves in the feared situation and, while watching the movie of themselves, to step out of themselves and stand several feet behind themselves. In other words, they will be behind themselves, seeing the back of their heads as they watch the movie. At this point the therapist will "collapse anchors" by touching both forearms. Since the brain cannot receive two conflicting messages, it opts for the pleasant one. It sends calm feelings rather than phobic ones. After this, to reinforce the change, clients thank the part of themselves that was afraid for giving themselves whatever benefit that part wanted them to have by being afraid.

The Emotional Transfusion tool, which I explained in my first book, is much like NLP. I never used to visualize the fear-causing events unless I saw myself in the movie (and I always saw myself as being completely relaxed and happy in that situation). However, NLP programmers do not always have their clients step out of themselves and watch the movie. Sometimes they advise clients simply to be present in the movie, alert to the five senses. Some people have told me that they had difficulty in seeing themselves in their visualizations. If you are one of these people, you might do as the NLP programmers sometimes do: Just be in the scene, without trying to see yourself as an actor in the movie.

If you are afraid to drive, for instance, visualize yourself in the car. Feel the texture of the steering wheel under your hands and the softness of the seat under your body. Smell the new-car odors. See the colors of the upholstery and the street scene through the windshield. Hear the motor turn over. At the same time, feel a sense of happiness and excitement, a feeling of competence at being able to drive. How do you do that? Like the NLP therapists, I believe you have to have a resource that will permit you to overcome your fear. That was why I advocated learning how to use what I called Emotional Transfusion. You could transfuse the resource you needed—the self-esteem and happy calm from one experience—into a visualization of a scene that ordinarily caused panic. With that resource, you could overcome fear.

With Emotional Transfusion I replaced the panicky feelings I used to have while making sales calls with the good and competent feelings I had when I once almost made a hole-in-one at Pebble Beach.

Emotional Transfusion works much like a blood transfusion. When I used it to overcome my anxiety about sales calls, I first went to alpha and created a *donor* visualization. I saw myself at Pebble Beach enjoying the beautiful scenery and atmosphere. Then I saw the happy look on my face when I almost hit a hole-in-one and I felt the jubilation. Next, retaining those feelings of confidence, I created my *receiver* visualization. I saw myself making the sales call, but I pictured myself with the same happy smile I had at Pebble Beach. I also saw my client's face looking just as pleased as I was. At the same time, I affirmed that I enjoyed making a sales call and being with this client. The surprising result was that my unconscious really did take over! My "boss" eliminated my anxiety, my feelings of inferiority, and my what-if's. I found myself enjoying the sales call. When I discovered that I actually liked the client and was interested in him as a person, I enjoyed the challenge of selling to him. I became much more successful.

While I still believe that visualizing works best if you can actually *see yourself* in the movie, I also believe that you can visualize effectively if you simply *experience* yourself as being in the movie. You also can adapt the NLP technique of anchoring to make Emotional Transfusion more effective. Touch your forearm when you have completed your donor visualization. Then, when you visualize yourself in the scene that causes your fear, touch your forearm again as a signal to your unconscious to send you feelings of calm and self-worth. Anytime you are feeling nervous or panicky, touch your forearm in the same way, and the calming feelings will return.

Your Alpha Goals

In your notebook, in the third FEAR-Smasher section, write down your goals for working this key. Here are some goals I would suggest:

1. Learn how to go to alpha.
2. If you are housebound, go to alpha six times a day, enjoying the calm of your secret resting place.
3. If you are not housebound, go to your secret resting place in alpha at least three times a day.
4. Practice your ability to visualize at alpha, by re-creating at least one different happy, jubilant, calming, or successful experience each day for a week.
5. When you have found the visualization that makes you feel best about yourself, anchor in this donor visualization by touching your forearm while you are experiencing it.
6. Practice your ability to make Emotional Transfusion work for you. I suggest that you use Emotional Transfusion to increase your feeling of self-worth before starting to work on a specific phobia.
7. Write out twenty affirmations about yourself.
8. Select the affirmations that you feel are most effective, and use them in conjunction with your visualizations.
9. Experiment with body therapy as a means of relaxation.
10. Learn to do abdominal breathing.

Does this key sound difficult? It might seem so at first. But once you learn to go to alpha, you will not have to make yourself go there. You will *want* to go. And once you've discovered the miraculous changes you can make with Emotional Transfusion, you will seek out ways you can use visualizations and affirmations to eliminate Mr. Negative from your unconscious.

CHAPTER
8

HOW MUCH CAN YOU RISK?

USAN B. ANTHONY was an American who wasn't afraid to risk. Incensed that only men could vote, she led a group of women who marched to the polls in Rochester, New York, in 1872. Arrested and convicted of having voted illegally, this indomitable woman refused to pay the $100 fine and was never required to. Although she herself was never able to vote legally, she and her sister suffragists risked ridicule and humiliation so that others eventually could enjoy the right to vote.

Susan B. Anthony refused to play the victim. She risked and didn't stop risking when others claimed that she had failed. Although she was denied the full rights of citizenship, she *acted as if she already had them* by challenging the male officials at the polls, lecturing throughout the nation, and even organizing an International Council of Women. Her actions brought her worldwide recognition in 1904.

Two letters I received one day made me think of Susan B. Anthony's remarkable ability to act as if she were already the way she wanted to be. Both came from young married women of similar backgrounds who had read *Anxiety and Panic Attacks*. Both had had panic attacks for several years and had tried "everything" to get over them.

Carla wrote:

> I've read your book and I liked it very much, but
> I still have an overwhelming fear that never

seems to leave me. I tell myself you can't die from a panic attack, *but I don't believe it. I tell myself that the attacks are a sure sign that I have some physical problem.* [italics added] The doctor says my only real problem is arthritis, but I keep having headaches, a rapid heartbeat, and constant pains in my shoulder and back. Something else just has to be wrong!

Lynne, the other woman, wrote:

I've had agoraphobia for the past five years and I can't tell you how invaluable has been your positive approach. Learning to think positively has been my main strength for being able to get out of the house and desensitize myself. Thanks for changing me from a phobic to a "freebic."

What is the difference between these two women? Carla is playing the victim. She's telling herself that something terrible is wrong with her. Her unconscious is taking it in and sending back paralyzing fear thoughts. This tyrannical "boss" prevents her from practicing relaxation, desensitization, and physical fitness routines.

Lynne not only has quit thinking negatively about herself but has developed her ability to risk. Her courage has paid off with freedom from fear.

The Fourth FEAR-Smasher Key

I formulated my fourth FEAR-Smasher key when I realized how many fearful people think and act like Carla.

The Fourth FEAR-Smasher Key: *Risk* developing your ability to attempt new things.

Risking means moving into the unknown. It means accepting that you can handle the unknown, no matter what situation comes up. It's Christopher Columbus, sailing into the uncharted ocean despite the dire predictions of all the doubters. It's Lee Iacocca, leading the Chrysler Corporation like a winner when to everyone else it looked like a loser.

Once I developed my ability to risk, I stopped playing the victim. Even though I was still afraid to leave my safe place, I started using the tools that would permit me to desensitize myself to my fear. First I programmed my unconscious boss to send me calm feelings. Then I set a goal of being able to go wherever I wanted without having a panic attack. Then I actually began leaving the house. I practiced approaching the supermarket. Then I entered it, and finally I was able to make some purchases. When the fear symptoms appeared, I accepted that they were there, but I told myself that they were simply a normal body response. I kept on going, doing more and more things away from home. Each little success reinforced the message I wanted to send to my brain that no longer was I afraid to leave my house. My unconscious then saw that the old fear symptoms were inappropriate. Eventually it sent me nothing but calm feelings.

Risking brought me other rewards, too. When I decided that I wanted to overcome my fear of public speaking so that I could help others overcome fears and phobias, I risked joining Toastmasters International. The result was a new and successful career as a professional speaker. When I wanted to become more physically fit, I risked running every day. Eventually I was able to run a half marathon, and I became healthier and calmer.

All of these risks paid off in successes for me. However, the purpose of risk-taking is not so much to aim for success as it is to understand that it's OK to try and fail and keep on trying. Most of us are afraid that if we take a risk and fail, it will somehow devastate us. "What will others think?" we worry. "It's safer not to try."

If this is your attitude, don't despair. Note that my fourth FEAR-Smasher doesn't say that the ability to risk is a God-given talent or a natural part of your personality. It says that you can *develop* your ability to risk.

In this chapter I am going to show you several ways to make

it easier to risk doing the things you must do to recover from irrational and rational fears. But first, let's review the Fourth Basic Principle I gave you in *Anxiety and Panic Attacks: Act as if you are already the way you want to be.* If you want to be free of fears and phobias, then act as if you already are this way. Tell yourself you are calm and relaxed while you are in the situation that frightens you.

It's easier to act *as if* when you make use of the alpha programming tool. When I visualized and affirmed at alpha that I was already free of fear and enjoying going to the supermarket, my unconscious didn't realize that I was merely rehearsing. It believed that I actually was at the supermarket feeling calm and happy. When I drove the car to the supermarket parking lot, my unconscious told me, "You've done this before. You don't have to be afraid." It then sent me feelings of calm.

Alpha programming followed by acting *as if* causes actual changes to take place in the brain. This is true because of the *law of association.* By acting *as if* you are already free of anxiety while you are in a fear-producing situation, you reinforce the experience of being calm. Message after message goes to your brain, and it finally associates calm rather than anxiety with the situation that frightens you.

Another law, *operant conditioning,* will work for you if you give yourself "attaboys" or "attagirls" for acting *as if.* This law states that human beings can be conditioned to change through a system of rewards for appropriate behavior. Your self-praise for acting *as if* will condition your unconscious to give up the fear habit.

The Ability-to-Risk Quiz

Take a moment to answer the following questions yes or no. Then see if your cognitions—what you are telling yourself about yourself—are standing in the way of acting *as if.* If so, write these cognitions in your notebook and counter them with helpful affirmations.

1. Can you accomplish something like a report or a term paper only if you have a deadline? If so, you are practicing *perfectionism*. You are so fearful of making a mistake that you won't risk doing the research required. You may also be doing *white-is-black thinking* if you are predicting that you are bound to do badly on the project. By putting off the hard work until the night before the project is due, you make certain of doing less than your best. You fulfill your worst expectations. Give yourself permission to do less than the world's most perfect job. Then act *as if* you are capable: Dig right in and start. No matter how you do, give yourself an "attaboy" or "attagirl" for having acted in a positive way. You'll condition yourself to have less fear of assignments the next time around.

2. When someone asks you to do something new, such as joining a club or going to a party, do you always say no? If so, you are guilty of *negative focusing*. You are seeing your irrational fears as unsurmountable barriers to enjoyable activities that could improve your self-image and lift depression. You can overcome negative focusing by refusing to say, "*What if* I have a panic attack while I'm in a social situation?" and countering with "*So what if* I have an attack? I can use calming tools and remain in the situation. If I have to leave, I can explain to others what is happening. I am a worthy person no matter what happens." Then go on and risk having some fun.

3. When you are among friends, do you give your opinions about the issues discussed, or do you go along with what others say even though you disagree violently? If so, you are practicing *rejectionitis*. You are so afraid that others will disapprove of you because you are "different" that you won't risk saying what you believe. Challenge this faulty cognition by telling yourself that it is not necessary that everyone think as you think. It is not even necessary that everyone like you. You are a person of worth no matter what others think. There are plenty of

people who do like you. If you are uncertain of this, make a list in your notebook of people who like you.

4. Do you avoid taking up golf, tennis, or some other enjoyable sport because you tell yourself that your racing heart, jelly legs, and hyperventilation make it impossible? If a doctor has proclaimed you healthy despite these symptoms, you are practicing *stretch-or-shrink thinking*. You are stretching the truth about your physical liabilities and shrinking the fact that your health is good despite your irrational fear symptoms. Go to alpha and see yourself having a good time participating in these sports. Affirm that you are perfectly healthy. Then go out and risk starting to enjoy your new hobby. Healthy activities like these will make your body more fit and you more relaxed. They also nurture the little child in you who really wants to have fun and to send you good feelings.

5. Have you refused to tell your husband that you have irrational fears and then blown up at him when he got irritated because you insisted that he do the weekly grocery shopping? If so, you are using *"should" and "ought" legalisms*. You're telling yourself your husband "should" understand your fears even when you haven't told him about them. You may also be making yourself feel guilty because you feel that you "ought" to be able to go to the supermarket. Risk telling your husband that you are afraid and asking his help. Affirm that you are a worthy person no matter what, and save yourself a lot of guilt, anger, and depressed feelings.

6. Have you given up trying to desensitize yourself because, after all, panic runs in your family and you might just as well get used to it? If so, you are practicing *mistaken identity*. You are playing the victim, telling yourself that you are a hopeless case because you tried and failed to overcome a phobia. Counter this thought with "I had to retreat the last time I tried, but I can try again. I can use

the tools I have learned for overcoming fear symptoms. They have worked for other people, and they will work for me." Risk giving yourself a compliment just for trying, and you will be surprised at how operant conditioning will make it easier for you to go out the next time.

7. When your spouse drinks too much and blames it on the fact that you have a panic disorder, do you tend to feel guilty? If so, you are practicing *"My fault!"* thinking—assuming the blame for your spouse's bad behavior. Counter this faulty cognition with "I am only responsible for my own behavior, not my spouse's. It's up to my spouse to solve the drinking problem." Then risk being assertive by telling your spouse you're not accepting the responsibility for his drinking, but you do love him and hope that he will seek help.

8. Your best friend wants to take you to a study group because she says you're an intelligent person who is a perfect candidate for the club. Do you tell her she's crazy, you never made a grade higher than a C, and then refuse? If so, you are *refusing the positives.* Go to alpha and build your self-esteem by affirming all the good things about yourself. The next time you receive a compliment or an invitation, risk accepting it.

9. It's your birthday and you remember that another year has gone by and you still have a terrible breathing problem that interferes with everything you do, yet your doctor says nothing is wrong physically. Do you tell yourself you must be suffering a nervous breakdown? If so, you are practicing *fictional fantasies.* You are letting your emotions substitute for the truth about what is happening. You are not crazy; you have a fear habit that can be overcome. Go to alpha and see yourself going places and enjoying it, completely free of breathing problems. Affirm that you are completely sane and that you deserve happiness. Then risk acting *as if* by practicing relaxation

and beginning to desensitize yourself to your fears of going places.

Taking the Risk of Finding a Support Person

I've already told you how alpha reprogramming makes it easier for you to risk the process of desensitizing yourself to your fears. Now I want to tell you about some other tools. The first one is simply this: Ask someone—your spouse, your parent, your child, or a friend—to help you.

You may be thinking, "Oh, no, I'm not going to tell the only person in the world who cares about me that I have irrational fears. Then I might be left with no one." If you take this risk, you might be happily surprised at the response. If you don't tell your spouse or other loved ones why you have been acting in such mysterious ways, they may think that you are being difficult, lazy, dominating, or unhelpful. Simply tell them that you have an irrational fear, that you want to work on getting over it, and that you would appreciate their help. If they have never heard of a phobia, give them this book to read.

It is important, however, to select a person who will be helpful and not harmful. Do not under any circumstances select someone who demands, "Snap out of it. It's all in your head." Even worse is the person who fusses and fumes that you're "hopeless" and destroys your self-esteem. At the other extreme are persons who are so solicitous that they try to do everything for you. They insist that the best thing to do when you feel fear is to lie down and let them wait on you. That would be harmful, not helpful.

Be sure that whoever you select gets some training in how to help a person with a phobia. If you are going to a therapist, ask the therapist to brief your support person. If you are not, ask your helper to read all the books you have read, including this one. Chapter 10 will tell your support person how to help you and respond to you as well as how to maintain his or her own equilibrium at the same time.

Just as water wings support children in the ocean until they can swim on their own, a good helper can support you while you are submerged in fear-producing situations. Your helper does not and should not shield you from the situation of which you are afraid; this person simply enables you to keep your head out of water while you are learning to enjoy it.

If you experience fear symptoms while you are exposing yourself to a feared situation, a good support person can say encouraging things to you. He or she can help you focus on nonthreatening thoughts, praise you lavishly for small successes, and counter the faulty cognitions you have about yourself with positive, rational statements. A good support person can be invaluable!

One way to work with a support person is to set aside an hour once or twice a week when you can work together on desensitization. If you are feeling afraid to try when the appointed hour arrives, your support person can give you encouragement to take the first step. If you have to retreat, he or she can praise you for having tried and encourage you to try again.

As the person being supported, you have some duties, too:

- Explain what you want your support person to do. Tell him or her to praise you for successes, encourage you to risk exposure, and give you positive cognitions about yourself.
- Don't expect the support person to do the work that you need to do. Your support person cannot take away fear symptoms. He or she can talk to you and use some of the tools I am going to give you in this chapter to help you experience the fear as less threatening.
- If your support person lives with you, don't expect that person to give up usual routines and stay at home with you if you are housebound. Everyone needs to live a normal life. Simply ask your support person to give you an hour or two a week and to encourage you whenever he or she is at home.
- If you are feeling angry that your support person doesn't help more, learn some communication skills so that you can assert yourself. In one study, the agoraphobics and

their spouses who were taught communication skills improved more quickly than the agoraphobics who were taught only relaxation techniques. Furthermore, they were able to resolve conflicts in the marriage better. They could say what they really felt. A good counselor can help you learn these skills.

• When you start getting better, reassure your support person that you will continue to care about him or her. Your support person may have had to take over most of the family duties because you were phobic. He or she performed these duties in a spirit of love. When you recover and take over your normal duties, your support person may interpret this action as a personal repudiation. Studies show that family counseling can help in these situations.

Taking the Risk of Desensitizing

If you are phobic, exposing yourself to the situation of which you are afraid doesn't have to be a terrible ordeal. You can use the same tools that therapists use to lessen the anxiety you feel when you risk desensitization. One way is to sit down with paper and pen and describe what is known as a hierarchy of fears. You do this by first ranking your sensations of fear on a scale of one to five. Next, on another sheet of paper, describe in nine or ten progressive steps how difficult it is to face your feared situation. Then rate the intensity of the fear symptoms you feel at each step. For instance, if you have a fear of flying, you might say that when you approached the airport you were feeling a "two," sweaty palms, but that when you were inside the plane, your feelings had escalated to a "four," difficulty in breathing.

By thinking about which *number* best describes your anxiety, you focus your mind away from the fear symptom at the time you feel it. You are saying, "I'm feeling a 'five,' " not "I'm going to scream! I'll lose control! What if I faint?" Whenever you reduce the harmful self-talk, your unconscious rewards you with calmer body sensations.

The hierarchy also allows you to compare how much better you are doing as you continue to expose yourself to the situations you fear. You will find the numbers dropping as you improve.

When you create your hierarchy, start by describing the worst symptoms. You will find it easier to work backward (and you'll end on a calmer note, too). Here is how a typical "fear sensation ranking" might look:

5. Panic	Disorientation, pounding heart, feeling that I am about to pass out
4. High anxiety	Difficulty in breathing; feel weak all over
3. Moderate anxiety	Stomach feels uncertain; pulse rate increases
2. Mild anxiety	Palms sweat; mouth feels dry
1. Minimal anxiety	Cold feet; warm face

Remember that people experience anxiety symptoms in different ways. Your description of your own symptoms could vary from the example.

Here is a typical "scale of difficulty in facing feared situations" for someone who fears going to the shopping mall. Each step is linked with the number of the anxiety symptom response:

Situation	Rating of Feeling
9. Being in the center of a noisy mall, cut off from exits by long hallways crowded with people	5 (Disorientation, etc.)

8. Waiting in line to pay for several items inside one of the stores — 5 (Disorientation, etc.)

7. Paying for one item inside a store — 4 (Difficulty breathing, etc.)

6. Looking for goods inside a store — 3–4 (Weak feeling, beginning to breathe hard)

5. Looking in shop windows in the center of the mall when crowds are sparse — 3 (Weak feeling)

4. Looking in shop windows on an aisle that has an exit in view — 2 (Sweaty palms)

3. Walking inside the shopping mall — 2 (Sweaty palms)

2. Standing outside the door — 2 (Sweaty palms)

1. Driving into the mall parking lot — 1 (Cold feet)

When you have made out your hierarchy of fears, show it to your support person. Ask your helper to remind you to focus on the numbers, not the feeling, if you begin to feel anxious while you are going into your anxiety-causing situation.

More Focusing Techniques

Arthur B. Hardy, M.D., helps his TERRAP clients to do either *inward* or *outward focusing* whenever they feel anxiety symptoms while exposing themselves to feared situations.

To do inward focusing, note what your fear symptoms are and then try to make them *worse*. For instance, if your hands are getting sweaty, try to make them even wetter. You will most likely not be able to make this happen. Many people who do inward focusing are pleasantly surprised to find the physical symptoms *disappearing* rather than growing stronger when they focus inward.

To do outward focusing while you are anxious, try to describe the clothes you are wearing, count the number of chairs in the room or trees in the yard, and note colors, smells, or textures. The point is to distract your mind from your fear symptoms by focusing on your surroundings rather than on fear thoughts.

Booting Out the Bogeyman

Dr. Richard O. Anderson, clinical assistant professor in psychiatry at the University of Minnesota, said at a workshop at the Seventh Annual National Conference on Phobias and Related Anxiety Disorders that phobics are in trouble with the bogeyman. They are accepting irrational explanations for the fear they feel. He advises his patients to ask themselves questions to determine the rational explanations for their fears.

As a recovered phobic, I heartily agree with both his diagnosis and his therapy. We phobics are telling ourselves that because we are afraid of a bridge or an elevator or an airplane, we are going crazy or that because we have a racing heart, we are going to have a heart attack. But feelings are not facts. They are nothing but the bogeyman, and if we are adults, we know there is no such thing!

You can boot the bogeyman out of situations in which you are afraid by talking to yourself in the right way. First, realize that whatever happens has both a rational and an irrational explanation. Determine which is the rational one, and tell yourself that that is what you will believe. You are going to believe in facts, not feelings!

Here are four questions to help you determine whether you are thinking irrationally and the rational answers you can adopt to challenge this destructive form of thinking:

- Do you see your fear symptoms as signs that something dreadful is about to happen? If the house is on fire, your panic is rational. If nothing unusual is going on, accept the rational explanation that you are merely nervous. Affirm that you have tools that will help you reduce the irrational symptoms.

- While you are having an attack, are you saying to yourself, "This is dangerous. I am either dying or going crazy"? Boot out this irrational bogeyman thinking by agreeing with yourself that the attack is distressing and uncomfortable but reminding yourself that you have been through attacks before and nothing serious happened.

- Are you constantly thinking that nervousness and panic are permanent conditions for you and that you just can't stand it another day? Challenge your irrational assumptions. Tell yourself that plenty of people, like Bob Handly, have completely overcome their anxieties and panic attacks. You can stand it, and you know that eventually you will recover.

- Do you dwell on your nervous stomach, your headaches, or your fast pulse? If you do this, you are allowing your irrational thinking to make your physical symptoms of anxiety worse. Commit yourself to rational thinking. Focus on new fitness routines or hobbies that can be fun. Replace your irrational thoughts with goals for the future.

In a recent stress management seminar I conducted, I urged the business executives who attended to find noncompetitive hobbies as a way of reducing stress. Afterward, Bill, a corporate officer who admitted he was something of a workaholic, told me, "I don't like to do anything if I can't keep score!"

If you are looking for a hobby as a means of overcoming nervousness, you don't need to join a tennis league or enter your model airplanes in a statewide competition. Your goal should be to relax, not to measure your accomplishments against others'. Bill finally elected to take up glider soaring, a sport he had always wanted to do but hadn't allowed himself time to develop. Now Bill loves the elation and calm he feels when soaring in the clouds: He doesn't have to compare himself with anyone else's progress to enjoy the sensations. His nervousness has been reduced, too.

The Risking Goal

In your notebook, write this goal: "I will develop my ability to risk." Then create short-term goals according to your own needs, using these five suggestions:

1. Write down five ways in which you will risk acting *as if.* (Think of five irrational ways you have been perceiving your fears, and write the rational and positive actions you will take to counter this kind of thinking. For instance, if you have been telling yourself that you can't go shopping because you are afraid you will get too nervous, counter this irrational perception with "I love to go shopping. Standing in line gives me a chance to relax.")

2. Write your pledge to go to alpha at least three times a day, and visualize and affirm yourself as a person willing and eager to risk desensitizing.

3. Write out a list of persons you could ask to be a support person. Write down what you will say to the person of your choice when you ask his or her help.

4. Write out your hierarchy of fears, rating the intensity of your feelings in each situation.

5. Write down the dates when you will work on desensitization for the next month. Leave space for writing in "attaboys" or "attagirls" for each date.

The Payoff of Risking

Robert Frost, the much loved American poet, wrote these lines about risking in his poem "Bravado":

Have I not walked without an upward look
Of caution under stars that very well
Might not have missed me when they shot and
fell?
It was a risk I had to take—and took.

From The Complete Poems of Robert Frost, published by Holt, Rinehart &
Winston. Reprinted by permission.

Frost himself risked when he refused to follow the experimentation of many twentieth-century poets. He took his inspiration from common life situations and expressed lyrical truths in the language of ordinary people. He risked, won the Pulitzer Prize four times, and lived a life of fulfillment in the rural New England that he loved.

You, too, must take a risk in order to walk without an upward look at your irrational fears, which hover over you like giant meteors threatening to fall. If you take it, however, you, like many others who have done so, can overcome those fears and lead a calm life of fulfillment.

9

THE MIRACLE KEY

W HEN MARILYN GELLIS discovered that her terrible "heart problems" were really agoraphobia, she became a new person. This Palm Springs, California, mathematics consultant and teacher hadn't been able to find anyone to help her recover, so she helped herself by reading everything she could find about phobias and panic disorder. She also made an important commitment. She vowed to turn her irrational fear into a source of strength that would nourish others who were afraid.

Then she pursued a Ph.D., doing her doctoral dissertation on agoraphobia. Next, she placed a three-line classified ad in the *Desert Sun*, a local Palm Springs newspaper, that read, "Anyone who has panic attacks or is afraid to go to the market, please call me." In the first week alone, she got 150 calls. When she held a meeting at her house, however, only five people were brave enough to leave their safe place and come. That didn't stop Marilyn. She made this handful of people the core of her Institute for Phobic Awareness, which offered therapy and a support group. Then, in 1986, Marilyn (now Dr. Gellis, an experienced therapist) purchased a three-bedroom home that she turned into an inpatient facility for severe panic sufferers. Many people in the community who, through her efforts, now understood what a panic attack was donated funds to help pay for the center, which opened toward the end of 1987.

Marilyn told members of the Phobia Society of America that she was fully aware of the miracle that took place when she championed the cause of wiping out agoraphobia.

"I named my residential recovery facility the Chrysalis Center, because when I was having panic attacks and no one seemed to be able to help me, I thought of myself as an ugly little worm with a terrible problem. But now I've emerged from my chrysalis, and I'm a free butterfly," she said.

By reaching out to others, Marilyn not only had the satisfaction of knowing that she helped other people overcome irrational fears; she found recovery for herself, and she developed a whole new career. Now she looks forward to the future with enthusiasm.

Marilyn is not alone in believing it is a special gift to know what irrational fears are and to recover from them. Many other people who have suffered from panic attacks or phobias have used those trying experiences as the very means of helping others. In doing so, they have benefited themselves.

The Fifth FEAR-Smasher Key

My fifth FEAR-Smasher key added a new dimension to the Five Basic Principles I developed for *Anxiety and Panic Attacks*. I used to believe that you acquired the desire to reach out to others after you had a Life Plus transformation. As I began to write *Beyond Fear*, however, I saw that *the cultivation of this desire was a therapeutic tool in itself.* If you didn't possess this key of wanting to help others, you could develop it. Then it would in turn strengthen your ability to overcome fear by increasing your feeling of self-worth.

> The Fifth FEAR-Smasher Key: Share the hope by reaching out to help others.

How does this key enable you to reduce irrational fears? If you have had a severe phobia or have been afraid to do the things that everyone else seems to do and enjoy, you are subject to depression. "What's the use of trying?" you may ask yourself. Instead of finding positive ways to work on your fears, you succumb to playing the victim.

What happens when you reach out to help someone else who has the same problem? You encourage that person to use the very tools you need to use. When you hear yourself giving others "attaboys" and helping others to think positively, *it is easier to motivate yourself to use the tools in spite of your own apathy.*

The first step in reaching out to others may be simply to inform others that there are such things as irrational fears and phobias. You can do this by opening up and sharing your experiences with others. Once you have found someone with similar problems, you can be a good friend by listening, encouraging, and praising their efforts to change.

How willing are you at this point to reach out to others? Answer the questions that follow to determine whether cognitive distortions are interfering with your ability to share with others.

The Reaching-Out Quiz

1. Do you tell yourself that it's impossible for you to reach out to others because you're too nervous or have too many headaches, a nervous stomach, or a rapid heartbeat?

If so, you are doing *stretch-or-shrink* thinking. Stretching the significance of your physical limitations is like putting a full bottle of water in the freezer. Pretty soon the water expands so much that it breaks the bottle. If you magnify your physical problems to the point of being inactive, you destroy yourself. Realize that there are lots of little ways you can begin to reach out to others, and by doing so, you'll grow rather than shatter yourself.

If your problem is that you are shrinking the value of the fearful experiences you have suffered, you are denying that you really do have a special gift to give to others.

In *Stepping Stones,* the newsletter of the support group PANIC, Inc., founder Betty Jaworsky wrote that she was housebound with agoraphobia in Scottsdale, Arizona, when she decided to organize the group. In only a few years this support group grew from a handful of people to a network of five groups in the Scottsdale area. In the beginning, she suffered anticipatory fear before each meeting, and she often told herself she was crazy to attempt such a thing. But the joy of having companionship with others like herself and the peace of mind of having someone to call on the telephone when her family was away gave her the motivation to continue. As Betty became more involved in helping others help themselves, she herself began to recover. Now she is able to work outside her home.

2. *Do you tell yourself that you can't reach out to others because you have too many family problems?*

If so, you are doing *negative focusing*. It is true that bickering, a marital separation, or problems with children are hard to take. But concentrating on the stressful things that happen to you only increases your stress. Focus instead on what you can do in spite of your problems.

Harry, a man who had been through all the trauma of a divorce and who had suffered with choking sensations for nine years, wrote to tell me that he was better. Not only was he working on the Five Basic Principles to overcome his panicky symptoms, but he was also reaching out to befriend another man going through a divorce. "I believe that if I can become involved in helping others, I can help myself," he wrote to me.

3. *Do you tell yourself that there's just no way that you can help someone else because you lack the educational credentials?*

If so, you are *refusing the positives* in your life. You are seeing your painful experiences with irrational phobias only as negatives. If you will let them, they can be a wonderful gift to others.

Mary Ann Miller, founder of Agoraphobics in Motion (A.I.M.) in Royal Oak, Michigan, started out as "just an agoraphobic." Now her self-help program, which includes the tools of Alcoholics Anonymous, has reached over 500 phobic people. Her experience as an agoraphobic and in helping others led to her becoming part of a team of scientists that has done research on the relationship of alcoholism to agoraphobia. Mary Ann, now licensed by the state to do counseling, presented the results of the research to the Phobia Society of America in 1986 (see Chapter 16).

4. *Do you tell yourself that you just aren't able to reach out to others because people are always putting you down?*

If so, you may be doing *white-is-black* thinking by interpreting someone else's actions as hostile to you when they merely indicate that person's own discomfort. Remind yourself that you are not the cause of everyone else's strange behavior and risk accepting people who seem hostile as they are.

A friend of mine whom I'll call Laura canceled out her white-is-black thinking when she sat down and thought rationally about why her friend Betsy always seemed angry. She realized that Betsy was having a hard time dealing with a death in her family and was not reacting to anything Laura had done. Laura took the first step in reaching out to Betsy by reading a book describing how to help a bereaved person. She invited Betsy to lunch and spent the hour listening to Betsy rage about everything and everybody. She didn't try to change Betsy's irrational thinking, but she did tell her she loved her. Betsy looked at her with tears in her eyes and told her she was the only person who seemed to understand. Laura took a risk in reaching out, but she did it. Her feeling of self-worth grew by leaps and bounds.

5. *Do you tell yourself that you can't reach out to others because you're too nervous to do anything socially with another person without taking a drink, and you don't want to drink any more than you have to?*

If so, you're practicing *mistaken identity*. You are telling yourself that you are all bad because you have made the mistake of becoming too dependent on alcohol. Affirm that you have gifts to give to others. You can help them without the crutch of alcohol. Reach out *while* you work on recovering from addictive drinking.

Almost everyone knows that Alcoholics Anonymous was founded by two alcoholics, stockbroker "Bill W." (William Griffith Wilson) and surgeon "Dr. Bob S." (Robert Holbrook Smith). These two friends found that they could maintain their sobriety through selfless service to other alcoholics. Since they founded AA in 1935, millions of other alcoholics have maintained their sobriety by practicing AA's Twelve Steps. One of the most cherished steps is the promise to attempt to carry the love and understanding they have found to others. If you have made a mistake in your life, realize that you can grow from it and that sharing your process of growing can help others.

6. *Do you tell yourself that you can't reach out to others because you're too angry about all the bad things that have happened to you due to the fact that you are prone to anxiety?*

If so, you are giving in to *fictional fantasies*. You are telling yourself that you *are* an angry, unloving person because you *feel* angry and that the only way that you can relate to others is to protect yourself from further hurt. Realize that your distorted thoughts only bring on more negative feelings. Alpha-program yourself with feelings of self-worth. Then go on and take the step to reach out.

In her autobiography, *You Can Too*, the late Mary Crowley told how she rejected the temptation to feel sorry for herself when she lost her job through no fault of her own back in 1957. She took the risk of acting in a positive way. She decided to found a company that would treat women the way she herself wanted to be treated. Then she worked tirelessly to build Home Interiors and Gifts into a multimillion-dollar direct sales company that gave housewives all over America a chance to grow financially. Through her unique style of sales training, she helped thousands to recognize their own self-worth. Because of her extravagant donations of money and time to worthy causes, she inspired countless others to begin to reach out, too.

How I Learned to Reach Out

If you don't know anyone else who admits to having irrational fears, your first step in working on the fifth FEAR-Smasher key is to find others who have irrational fears. You can do this easily by joining a support group for anxious people. Be a sharing, giving member in such a group, and you are bound to improve yourself.

That is exactly what happened to me. When I decided I wanted to overcome the number one fear in America (public speaking), I joined Toastmasters International. I quaked and shook when I made my first speech, but I felt very proud of myself when others praised me for having spoken before them at all when I was afraid. I kept going back. To fulfill my duties as a member, I began to evaluate others' speeches in a positive and encouraging manner. To my surprise, I saw that my comments actually helped others improve! I was so excited about my progress and the growth I helped bring about in others that I decided to reach out a little farther. I became president of the club and went on to spend many hours helping to create new Toastmasters groups in the Dallas area. All of this reaching out helped me increase my feeling of self-worth and encouraged me in my new career as a public speaker.

After I joined the Phobia Society of America, I took an active part with Jim Wilson of the Phobia Centers of the Southwest in forming a phobia support group in Dallas. Later we helped six other cities in the Southwest start support groups. Not only did I feel very good about having helped a lot of people who were trying to recover as I did, but my self-esteem was enhanced as well.

After the publication of *Anxiety and Panic Attacks*, I was besieged by phone calls from people who at last realized what was wrong with them and wanted support. By taking the time to share with these people one on one, I benefited in several ways. Listening to their problems reminded me to keep using the tools to keep myself in good shape. When they thanked me for listening, I increased my feelings of self-worth. Besides, talking with other people generated many new ideas for making the FEAR-Smasher keys more effective. By reaching out, I became able to help even more people through the publication of my book. The more people I could help, the more I could grow.

If you are not already in a support group of some kind, I urge you to join. Even if you are housebound, some groups have outreach programs. They will put you in touch with persons who will share with you by telephone or through letters. As you let others reach out to you and reciprocate with them, you will be amazed at how much easier it will become for you to work on overcoming fears.

Finding Your Own Support Group

How do you find a support group to join? Hundreds of people have written me asking for referrals to support groups, and there are probably hundreds of groups that would welcome you as a member. Many, like Emotions Anonymous and Recovery, have national affiliations. Others are strictly local, and the only way to find them is to check with sources in your area.

Look in the Yellow Pages under "Associations" and see if any of them might apply to irrational fears. If you are working with a therapist, ask if he or she knows of such a group or might be willing to form one made up of recovering clients. In forty-five cities, there are regional Self-Help Clearing Houses that might refer you to an established support group or help you form your own. (If your city doesn't have such a clearinghouse, contact the National Self-Help Clearing House, Graduate School and University Center, 33 West 42nd Street, New York, NY 10036, for information for your area.) Libraries often have listings of organizations by area of interest. The local Mental Health Association is also knowledgeable about such organizations. Ask your clergy member if local churches have such support groups.

You can also find a listing of support groups by state in the Phobia Society of America's *National Phobia Treatment Directory*. To order your copy, contact the Phobia Society of America, 133 Rollins Avenue, Suite 4B, Rockville, MD 20852. In 1987, the cost of this directory was $4 for members and $5.50 for nonmembers.

Forming Your Own Support Group

If you have checked all the possibilities and cannot find a support group, work the fifth FEAR-Smasher key: Reach out to others by forming your own group. It's really not so hard, as many phobic people can tell you. Many, like Marilyn Gellis, were off and running simply by placing a classified ad in a local newspaper to invite others who have problems with irrational fear to telephone them. One man I know, the husband and support person of an agoraphobic, asked local newspapers for a free public service ad and got something even better—a story in the newspaper about his desire to form a group. The response was impressive. Months later, people were still calling to say that they had read the story and wanted to participate in his group.

An easy way to start is to have the meetings at your home. Just share experiences with each other. As your group grows, you may want to have more structure to the meetings. You can decide whether you want outside speakers to come in, whether you will charge dues, have a newsletter, or sponsor social activities that can double as exposure work. You may want to explore together some nutritional and fitness tools for overcoming anxiety, too.

If you would like to start your own group, help is available. Here are some possibilities:

- Take advantage of the experiences of other groups in structuring your own. The Phobia Society of America no longer has local chapters that combine self-help and support activities with public education. It does, however, provide a number of resources, available through the PSA national office, to aid in forming a local support group. You can also write to the established support groups in the PSA directory for their advice and a subscription to their newsletter. Reading what others are doing can generate ideas for you.

- Professionals who specialize in treating clients with irrational fears are often eager to share their thoughts about how their therapies benefit clients. Members of your group can gain important information in this way.

- Make use of the "supermind" that is created when two or more people gather together to explore ideas for improvement. The value of a support group is that there is strength in numbers. In my own experience with support groups, I have discovered that when people share ideas about solving problems, creative ideas result. It is almost as if a separate group mind forms and comes up with the ideas. As your group creates its own supermind, answers to the questions of what to do and how to do it will be answered creatively.

It is also wise to recognize some of the pitfalls to avoid. Here are some to consider:

- Recognize that forming a support group can take a considerable amount of time. If you are willing to reach out to others by listening and sharing, your telephone will ring frequently, and your line will be busy many hours. If you cannot give away hours of your time, you may need to find someone else who can. You will also be reaching out if all you do is find the person who can lead the group. If you have the time to talk on the phone for hours but aren't willing to, consider doing it anyway. Remember that reaching out is one key to recovery for you. You will very likely enjoy talking to others with similar experiences, and you will grow as they offer you support and encouragement.

• Do not let the meetings become a place to share "war stories" about the symptoms of irrational fear. We who are prone to anxiety are quick to pick up symptoms we have never heard about before and make them our own. The emphasis of the meeting should be positive. Members should share ways of developing coping skills. For instance, Marilyn Gellis's group never speaks about a specific symptom, such as a nervous stomach or hyperventilation. Instead, members are encouraged to tell about how they have attempted to work on their problem. If they experienced fear, they describe it in terms of the numbers on their hierarchy chart (see Chapter 8). An assertive leader should be in charge, to remind those who simply want to complain about their symptoms that the support group is not the place to do it.

• Have enough structure so that members will talk about their avoidance behavior and the positive things they are doing to overcome it. However, allow enough flexibility so that shy members will not be afraid to share.

• Recognize that in small groups, cliques are likely to form. The people who form cliques may not intentionally want to cut other people out. They may simply band together and relate mostly to each other because they have a similar problem, such as an unsupportive spouse or difficulties with children. The effect on those who are not in the clique, however, can be harmful. If a clique becomes too strong, you may want to suggest that the persons in it form their own separate support group.

• Realize that visitors to an established group may feel shy. Appoint someone to give them special attention. In the Agoraphobics in Motion groups in Michigan, for instance, visitors are invited to sit at a "first-time table" where they can ask questions and become oriented before participating as members.

• Don't try to finance the group on your own. Most people will willingly pay dues to cover the costs of newsletters, invitations, and refreshments. Members may elect to contribute to a scholarship fund for people who really can't afford to pay.

- Recognize that a group should be split into two groups when it becomes too large for members to feel comfortable about talking and sharing. Most support group leaders say that the ideal size ranges from five to ten people who are regular attenders. When as many as fifteen to twenty people show up for meetings, the group should split.

The Reaching-Out Goal

A letter to PANIC's newsletter *Stepping Stones* tells how one agoraphobic member felt about the value of reaching out.

> Reaching out is a "scary" experience for me, but I find myself doing it again and again without even realizing it. A simple "hello" or a smile is reaching out. So is a telephone call to someone who themselves may also be afraid to reach out. Being willing to share your feelings, or listening to someone else's, is another way to reach out. No really great effort has to be taken. And any experience I had that I termed "frightening," I didn't have to look on as failing, because at least I tried and that's always a step in the right direction. For me, just recognizing this has enabled me to get in touch with my own feelings about reaching out. Being aware of the many different ways to reach out to someone and still be "safe" was a first step for me in realizing that I had something to offer. Reaching out is contagious— and it seems to create a chain that goes on and on.

You can start small with reaching out and get big results. But you have to take the steps to do it. Here are some things you can write in your notebook to help you take that important first step:

1. On one page, write this heading: "My Reaching-Out Goal." State the goal as follows: "I commit myself to risking new ways of thinking and acting in order to learn to reach out to others."

2. Under your short-term goal of going to alpha three times a day and reprogramming yourself, write down ten ways you can visualize and affirm yourself as reaching out to others. Be specific. Name names, describe situations. Here are some sample affirmations:

   - I enjoy reaching out to others by listening to them on the telephone.
   - I enjoy reaching out to others through sharing my experiences in a positive way.
   - I enjoy talking about the coping skills I have learned in this book.
   - I am happy to be a loving, caring person.
   - I am growing through my desire to reach out to _____.

   After you have formulated your affirmations, write how you will visualize these affirmations. See yourself calling someone on the phone, and then listening to that person. See yourself practicing acts of love for specific others— spouse, children, friends. See yourself looking happier and more relaxed while you are talking to them.

3. Make a short term goal of acting *as if.* Here are some suggestions:

   - I will make inquiries about finding a support group.
   - If I can't find a support group, I will put an ad in the paper and invite others who have irrational fears to telephone me.
   - I will make a special effort to reach out to _____ by doing these things: _____.

Remember, these are only my suggestions. You are a unique person with special gifts that you can share. Perhaps you are a good cook and could make a delicious dish to take to someone who is feeling depressed. Maybe you sew or sing or can type letters for someone. You have countless gifts besides the gift of having experienced irrational fears and learning to overcome them. Start small, but make a start. Do all that you can and you will grow faster than you believed possible.

PART

III

THE SUPPORT PERSON'S ROLE

CHAPTER

10

MESSAGE TO A
SPECIAL PERSON

I F SOMEONE has asked you to be a support person by helping that person get over a phobia, this chapter is especially for you.

First of all, I want you to know how important you are in helping your anxious relative or friend. (To simplify things, I'll refer to him or her as "your partner," using the masculine gender, from now on.) You have a tremendous influence for good when you support your partner in the right way. But if you try to "help" by overprotecting your partner or by encouraging him to avoid the things of which he is afraid, you can unfortunately have a tremendous influence for bad.

My former wife, Cindy, didn't know that she was functioning as a support person when I had agoraphobia, but she did fulfill the role. Instinctively she did a lot of things right. I will always be grateful to her that she never told me, "Snap out of it, Bob. You can go to the office if you try," or, even worse, "It's all in your head. You're just a hopeless case." Although we didn't understand what agoraphobia was, she was sympathetic. She didn't heap criticism on me and reinforce the guilt I already felt about not being able to do normal things.

Now that I know more about phobias, I have learned that support persons can take an even more active role. As well as providing unconditional love, they can help their partners desensitize themselves to whatever they fear. The support person who helps in the right way is like a mother bird. She builds a soft and loving nest in which to care for her babies. She feeds them, loves them unconditionally, and nurtures them. But when it is time for them to learn to fly and leave the nest, she starts gently nudging them out. If, when trying to fly, the baby birds fall down, she doesn't pick them up and put them back in the nest. Even though she may hate to see them struggling so hard, she lets them struggle. But she also keeps on flapping her wings, showing them how to fly and encouraging them to try again and again. If they keep on trying despite their difficulties, they eventually learn to transport themselves to the places where the most delicious bugs and worms are easy to find. They have the joy of being able to forage for themselves and to soar in the heavens. As long as they need it, however, they can return to the nest for the mother bird's love and attention.

The mother bird is the ideal role model for you. If you are an effective support person, you nudge your partner to expose himself to the very place or situation that holds terror. In a loving manner, you urge him to practice desensitization. First you go with him; then you gradually encourage him to expose himself to the feared situation on his own. You reward him with praise for all his efforts. You love him in spite of failures, but when he fails, you let him struggle. You *never reinforce his avoidance behavior* by telling him that you will go to the store for him or drive for him. You never suggest that because he is afraid, he should avoid making a speech or going to a party or entering a tall building. If you do your job well, you will simply accept the fact that your partner is afraid, avoid criticizing him for it, but go on nudging, praising, and loving.

The first thing you can do to prepare for being the right kind of support person is to read all of this book so that you can understand what a phobia is and how people can use the FEAR-Smashers to get over their fears. If your partner is in therapy, ask his therapist to make suggestions to you.

You're Special

You should feel complimented if your partner has asked you to be a support person. The invitation means that your partner trusts you, feels secure with you, and believes in you. He thinks you are special! In fact, Jim Wilson, of the Phobia Centers of the Southwest, says that a good support person can provide better help in the desensitization process than professionals. Because your partner has emotional ties with you, you have more influence over his behavior and feelings than his therapist does. And since you know him better, you know about any special difficulties your partner might have as he tries to expose himself to feared situations or places.

Of course, being a support person takes lots of work, patience, and fortitude, but the rewards are great. Whatever sacrifices you may have to make to help your partner, you can have the satisfaction of knowing that your efforts count in helping another person in very real ways.

Perhaps you are thinking, "I'm not a saint. Sometimes I really get angry that my partner has made life miserable for me and the rest of the family. I just can't understand how he could really be that afraid of something that isn't scary at all to me. It looks to me as if you have to be practically perfect to be a good support person. I'm just not that way." If these are your feelings, here are some tips for you:

- Realize that it's acceptable to feel angry from time to time. Just as an agoraphobic can't help feeling frightened about leaving the house, it is natural for you to experience the emotion of anger. Admit to yourself that you are angry, and talk it out with someone other than your partner. Then learn how to use the relaxation techniques I teach in the FEAR-Smashers for yourself.

- Avoid telling yourself, "I *should* be able to cure my partner. If I do everything *perfectly*, he'll be OK." If you have this attitude, you are thinking in irrational *"should" and "ought"* *legalisms* and practicing *perfectionism.* Use the cognitive restructuring techniques in the second FEAR-Smasher key for yourself. Affirm that you are a loving person and that it is OK for you or your partner to fail. It is not necessary for you to be perfect. Recognize that although you have pledged to help, your partner is responsible for his own progress.

• Make time in your life for yourself as well as for your partner. If your partner is your spouse and he has been housebound, he may have relied on you to do everything outside the house that needed to be done. At the same time, he may have expected you to fulfill all his social needs by staying around the house as much as possible. If you give in to these unspoken demands, you will only reinforce your partner's dependency. Remember that you don't have to be housebound, too. Develop hobbies and activities outside the home, even if your partner cannot participate in them. It will be better for both of you if you maintain your own separate identity.

• Start thinking of your partner as having an identity that is separate from that of the agoraphobic or of the one who has panic attacks. If this is difficult, try remembering what he used to be able to do. Plan some fun activities that have nothing to do with the phobia. Make a list of all your partner's good qualities and talents, and review it at times when you feel distanced or put off by your partner's problems.

Helping Your Partner Plan

Your first step in helping your partner expose himself to a feared place or situation is to sit down and talk. What does your partner expect of you? How can you help?

Even though your partner may really want to desensitize himself, remember that it is very frightening for him to do so. Together you should talk about the steps you will take in desensitizing. Help your partner construct a hierarchy of his fears (see Chapter 8). Write down specific goals that you want to achieve. Listen to how your partner feels. He will be able to judge better than you the relative difficulty of each goal.

Of course, every person's goals will be different, but here is a list of progressively difficult tasks that Jim Wilson suggests for agoraphobics:

1. Go together to a large store or supermarket during a time of day when it is least crowded. While inside, leave each other briefly.
2. Go together and wait outside while your partner shops inside.
3. Go together. Let your partner shop inside while you go elsewhere for an agreed-on length of time. Gradually increase the length of time you will be away.
4. Your partner goes shopping alone and returns alone. While shopping, he visits all areas of the store.
5. Repeat these exercises at a busy time.

Here is a suggested pattern for desensitizing by taking walks:

1. Walk together to the farthest point from home that your partner can manage. Stay for a short while before turning back.
2. Do the same thing while you follow a short distance behind.
3. Walk in a circular path, with each of you going in opposite directions and passing in the middle.
4. Walk separately by different routes and meet at the farthest point away from home. Make sure that you both understand where the meeting place will be and that you arrive first.
5. Your partner begins walking before you do and meets you later at an agreed-on place.
6. Your partner walks alone while you remain at home, increasing the distance of his walk daily.
7. Your partner walks alone while you are away from home, gradually increasing the distance.

Your partner should practice each of these steps several times before progressing to the next. He does not have to be completely free of fear while working on one step before attempting a more difficult one.

Helping Your Partner Make Exposure Trips

Remember that although your partner is serious about desensitizing himself, he really is terrified. Your role is to encourage him to make the effort when he is afraid to do it, and when he experiences anxiety or panic, to distract him from his fear and encourage him not to retreat. Here are some things you can do:

- If you notice that your partner seems tense or that he is rushing, talking, or breathing too quickly, encourage him to slow down. Talk about things you know might interest him. Look in display windows, admire flowers, note interesting signs. Find upbeat things to talk about.

- If your partner begins to be frightened by a strange feeling, do not encourage him to talk about his symptoms. Your partner should refer to his feelings only by the numbers he gave to his symptoms when he wrote out his hierarchy of fears. Accept the fact that he is feeling fear, but try to help him refocus. Try not to leave. Find a place to sit down or walk back a little way and rest. Don't get into lengthy discussions about panic feelings, but remind him that the symptoms are not dangerous, that he has had them before, and that they will pass. Talk about something else until your partner looks and behaves as if he is feeling better. Then go on practicing a little more before you go home.

- If it is impossible to stay in a place until the fear dies down or if the panic happens when your partner is alone, accept the fact that such "relapses" happen and praise your partner for having tried. Then nudge your partner to go back to the same place as soon as possible. If your partner is not able, you may notice a setback in the progress he has made in working on other goals as well.

When this happens, simply practice for a while on easier goals; then continue progressing.

Helping Your Partner by Giving Him an Out

Jerilyn Ross, M.A., associate director of the Roundhouse Square Psychiatric Center, Alexandria, Virginia, believes that phobics need to feel that they are in control of themselves and of their environment in order to expose themselves to a feared situation. The more they *feel* they are in control, the less anxious they will be. She advises asking your partner what he would like you to do to help him feel more comfortable. Then promise that you will do it, if it is at all possible.

Another way the support person can make his partner feel in control, Ross says in *Learning Theory Approaches to Psychiatry*, is to let the phobic know that he has the option of leaving a feared situation if he wants to. For instance, you could promise your partner before you buy theater tickets that even if he wants to leave during the middle of the performance, you will go with him. Paradoxically, your partner will be more willing to expose himself to a feared situation if he knows he has an out. Since he has control, he need not feel trapped.

Helping Your Partner by Praising and Rewarding

For phobics, exposure trips are hard work. Sometimes your partner experiences panic, sometimes boredom. Eventually your partner may equate desensitization with punishment and tell himself, "It's just not worth the effort." The only way to overcome this attitude is to associate pleasant things with desensitization. This process is called reinforcing, and you do it with praise and rewards. Here are some tips:

1. Whenever your partner makes the effort to desensitize, show that you are pleased.
2. If your partner is practicing alone, always ask how he got along. Be pleased with progress. Throw your arms around your partner and tell him you love him.
3. Don't complain about setbacks. Remind your partner

that he deserves an "attaboy" for trying and for continuing to try.

4. Post a list of exposure goals on a bulletin board and give your partner a red star for every one that he has achieved.

5. Give your partner a gift (not necessarily expensive) each time he has accomplished one of the goals. If you have been in the habit of bringing your partner small gifts anyway, make sure now that you give them only when progress is being made.

6. Give your partner points for each effort made, and special points for progressing to each new step. Allow your partner to trade a certain number of points for time off from doing certain chores (be sure they are not things he fears doing). Or agree that when your partner has accumulated enough points, you will shop together for that major appliance or piece of furniture that you have been planning to buy.

Helping Your Partner by Nudging

Only your partner can make the final decision about when he is ready to progress to a new desensitization goal, but you may need to encourage him to risk. When you judge that your partner is ready to progress, make a firm suggestion about what the two of you might do.

If your partner hesitates, reassure him by making several alternative arrangements to fall back on in case of difficulty. For instance, suggest that your partner walk alone, but remind him that you are available at home by telephone. (If he calls and tells you he is having a panic attack, help him overcome the disorientation he feels by refocusing his attention on his surroundings. Have him describe the clothes he has on, count the pages in the phone book, or tell you what is going on around him.)

You may also have to nudge your partner to do things alone in order to prevent him from being too dependent on your presence. If he makes excuses that he can't work on desensitization because he has letters to write or a home repair to make, suggest firmly that he put that chore aside for a while and try anyway. If he says that walking makes him fatigued, suggest that he practice regular exercises at home. (If he has been housebound a long time, walking probably does fatigue him!)

Here are some ways you can nudge constructively:

1. Don't allow anything to be mail-ordered or delivered that you can shop for. Instead, plan a pleasant shopping expedition for your necessities.
2. Encourage your partner to visit friends and go to the hairdresser, the dentist, or the doctor by preparing the way. Inform the persons to be visited that your partner might feel unwell and have to leave. By giving your partner this permission to walk out of a situation, he will have less need to do so.
3. Encourage your partner to take a job or do volunteer work. These activities hold their own rewards in increased self-confidence and perhaps even a paycheck. If possible, encourage your partner to use any money earned to buy something for himself.
4. If it is necessary to continue to practice on a single goal for a long time, alter the route or the time of day to prevent boredom.

Helping Yourself When Your Partner Improves

At last your partner shows improvement. He is beginning to do all the shopping and car-pooling, which used to be your exclusive chores. He may become active in a support group in which you don't participate, or he may go back to work. Suddenly, your own life falls apart. You may feel confused and left out. It seems as if now your partner just does not love you as he used to.

Perhaps you feel angry. "Why couldn't my partner have gotten over this phobia a long time ago? Just look at all the wasted years we have had," you tell yourself. The thought makes you depressed.

If you have feelings like these, *don't deny them*. The feelings may be only temporary, but they may also cause big problems for you and your partner if you don't address them. You have spent a great deal of effort helping your partner; now it is time for you to give yourself some well-deserved attention. Here are some tips for you:

1. Talk about your feelings with your partner. If communication is difficult, take a course or get some counseling in communication skills.
2. Plan some activities that you enjoy, and devote to these activities the time you formerly spent helping your partner.
3. Use cognitive restructuring (Chapter 6) to overcome feelings of *rejectionitis* or *fictional fantasies*. Write a list of twenty-five good things about yourself.
4. Spend time at alpha, visualizing and affirming yourself as having worth outside your role as a support person.
5. Continue to tell your partner that you love him.
6. Reach out to others. If you have successfully helped your partner to recover, you have learned skills that most people don't have. You have demonstrated patience, unconditional love, and acceptance. The world has need of your qualities. If you continue to give them freely to others, you will receive love in return. As both you and your partner develop your own special gifts, your relationship will grow better than you ever believed was possible.

Part

IV

Using the
FEAR-Smasher Keys

11

HOW TO USE THE FEAR-SMASHERS TO DO AWAY WITH SOCIAL PHOBIAS

I N PART II I explained in detail what the FEAR-Smasher keys were. In the next few chapters, I will show you how to apply the keys to specific kinds of rational and irrational fears. I will start with the social phobias—the fear of entering social situations—because they are so prevalent.

Even world-famous people have had to battle against social phobias. In a 1985 PBS documentary titled *Olivier: A Life*, Laurence Olivier told viewers that stage fright suddenly hit him after years of starring roles in famous plays. And world-class pianist Lorin Hollander said at a Southern Methodist University seminar on stage fright in 1987 that sweaty palms, dry mouth, and beads of perspiration on the brow are symptoms suffered by most performers. People who expose themselves to an audience learn ways to cope with the fear that they feel and go on with the show.

But stage fright isn't the only social phobia. If the fear that others will notice almost any particular action causes you to have sweaty palms or a queasy stomach or maybe even a full-blown panic attack, you are suffering from a degree of social phobia.

A social phobia like stage fright may not seem important if you aren't required to go on the stage. After all, who has to know that the sight of all those eyes fixed on you causes your heart to pound, your breathing to come nearly to a halt, and your mind to become disoriented? You can simply avoid the stage and go on being as normal as anyone else.

Millions of Americans have a diagnosed social phobia. Countless others are closet sufferers. If you are one of these millions, you may feel "perfectly normal," except that you just avoid making presentations in front of other people or you don't consider eating alone in a restaurant. Nor do you travel solo on vacation. If you're a social phobic contemplating marriage, you may so fear your partner's discovering the "real you" that you put off marching down the aisle to the altar.

Though it may be relatively easy to avoid the interactions with others that cause your body to express fear, who wants to? I know of lawyers whose careers are wrecked because they won't appear in court, beautiful women who wear unstylish clothes because they "can't" sign their name to a check or a charge slip in front of a clerk, intelligent children who fail in school because they are too nervous to sit in class. Yes, we can avoid the discomforts of social phobias, but we pay a price.

How do we get that way? Scientists tell us that we social phobics usually have physical, social, and psychological vulnerabilities to anxiety. If we don't protect ourselves against them, we allow our unconscious to be trained negatively. Then certain situations bring on anxiety or panic whether we like it or not.

With our nervous unconscious bossing us around, it is almost as if we are locked into a cage that prevents us from doing the things we want to do. But we don't have to stay there. By using the FEAR-Smasher keys, we can train our unconscious boss to react positively rather than negatively, and he will begin to send us calm feelings during anxiety-producing situations. We can leave our cage forever and go on to accomplish the great things that our social phobias formerly prevented us from doing.

My Experience with Social Phobias

You don't have to have agoraphobia to be a social phobic. In fact, studies show that half the people who have a public speaking phobia have no other mental health problem. I did have agoraphobia, but it wasn't until I had conquered it that I committed myself to getting over my phobia about public speaking.

Looking back, I believe that the reason I trembled and became disoriented when I tried to give a speech was that I gave in to *rejectionitis* thinking.

"What will happen if my nervousness causes me to give a poor speech?" I used to ask myself. "I'll be humiliated. Others will make fun of me. I'll be such a laughing stock that no one will ever want to associate with me again."

This was irrational thinking, and I knew it. But at that time my self-worth was so low that I didn't believe I could think any other way. My speech wasn't the only thing that I thought was below par. I, *myself*, wasn't good enough, and I was convinced that others were going to find out!

I first experienced the fear of public speaking as a child. In the third grade, I went through a lot of change. I moved to a different city, entered a new school, had surgery to correct a clubfoot, and then wore a cast on my leg for three months. After the cast was gone, I still felt conspicuous and sensitive about my leg. One day in the fourth grade, I had to give a book report in front of the class. Suddenly, all I could think of was, "Everybody is staring at me. They're thinking, 'There's that little crippled kid.'" I started to tremble. Someone laughed. I blushed and stammered. The book report was a disaster.

That one embarrassing experience was enough to program my unconscious to send me fear thoughts whenever I even contemplated giving any other reports. I started focusing on the part of me that felt conspicuous to others. I started telling myself that I "couldn't" give a report without being nervous, and sure enough, my body sent me fear reactions.

Years later, after I joined Toastmasters, I attacked this irrational fear psychologically, physically, and socially. I programmed myself at alpha to believe that no matter how many mistakes I made in giving a speech, I, personally, was still OK. Through the positive feedback I received from club members, I reestablished my perception that I did have self-esteem. At the same time, I learned how to write and deliver a good speech, and I gradually desensitized my body to the fear of standing before an audience. I gave myself "attaboys" every time I spoke in front of others.

Why You Have Social Phobias

If you have a social phobia, you most likely have special vulnerabilities that make your body more sensitive than other people's to anxiety-producing situations. The stress that a "normal" person takes in stride causes you to experience trauma (as I did when giving my book report). Your body, recognizing danger, fires off a fight-or-flight response. Then your psychological and social vulnerabilities come into play, reinforcing your fear. You tell yourself that you are scared and that there's something shameful about that. Other people will *know* that you are scared. By giving in to these vulnerabilities, you *train yourself to have a phobia*.

Here are the vulnerabilities to which you are subject:

- *Biological vulnerability.* For some people, shyness is a precursor of social phobias. Electrocardiograms done on shy children show that their hearts beat in a pattern that varies from the normal. The heart rate is elevated and does not vary with respiration. These and other physical differences are thought to cause such children to freeze when put in an unfamiliar situation. At a party, they stand at the side of the room longer before interacting with other children. They may also avoid eye contact.

  Social phobics have also been tested and found to have a greater surge of adrenaline when placed in anxiety-producing situations with others. Since adrenaline is the hormone that causes the fight-or-flight sensations, social phobics are born with a more sensitive trigger to anxiety. In addition, social phobics have a special sensitivity to stimulants, such as caffeine. The cup of coffee that you drink to "settle your nerves" may only increase your fear symptoms.

- *Social vulnerability.* If you are a social phobic, you tend to see your relationship to your peers as overly important. If you are placed in a very competitive situation, perhaps at work or in a school setting, this vulnerability may be heightened. Regardless of where you are, you are especially sensitive to what others think of you.
- *Psychological vulnerability.* If you are socially phobic, you probably do not recognize your self-esteem. Your ego may have become impoverished as a child if your parents praised you only for accomplishments, if they made you feel that you humiliated them in some way, or if your parents were alcoholic or had other problems with addictive behavior and gave you mixed messages about your self-worth. You may decide that it's safer not to try to do the things that make you anxious. You magnify the importance of what others may say about you, and you fear rejection. "After all," you tell yourself, "I made a fool of myself once before when I tried to make a speech or travel alone or eat by myself in a restaurant. What will happen if I do it again?" As you participate in this kind of damaging self-talk, you increase the adrenaline that is already flowing in your veins. You finally come to the decision that the only solution is to avoid that activity because you're just "too nervous" to do that kind of thing.

Using the Five FEAR-Smasher Keys to Overcome Social Phobias

You may have special vulnerabilities that make it easier for your unconscious to lock you into the cage of social phobias, but you also have the tools to fool Mr. Negative. By using the five FEAR-Smasher keys, you can do all of the following:

1. Set your goal to overcome your phobia and commit yourself to action (FEAR-Smasher Number One).
2. Resist the effects of your psychological vulnerability by calling in Mr. Positive, using cognitive restructuring, increasing your perception of worthiness, and nurturing your little child (FEAR-Smasher Number Two).
3. Through alpha programming, body therapy, and Emotional Transfusion, use your unconscious to reduce the fear symptoms generated by your body (FEAR-Smasher Number Three).
4. Increase your ability to risk desensitizing yourself through acting *as if,* using focusing techniques, and finding a support person (FEAR-Smasher Number Four).
5. Enhance your self-worth by reaching out to others (FEAR-Smasher Number Five).

FEAR-Smashing the Phobia of Public Speaking

Willard Scott, NBC-TV's national weatherman, has been quoted as saying that he frequently has symptoms of panic attack prior to going on the air. When he appeared on a nationally televised program on phobias, he had a hard time convincing other panelists that a public speaking phobia was a lot worse than having a few "butterflies in the stomach." It is difficult for nonphobics to believe that you can have tachycardia (pounding heart), hyperventilation, shaking legs and voice, and disorientation at the mere *thought* of having to speak before others. You don't even have to go before an audience to have it. You can feel this way even if you're communicating with only one other person who makes you nervous.

Dr. Philip G. Zimbardo, psychologist and author of *Shyness,* estimates that fully 40 percent of all Americans have a public speaking phobia, yet few seek help for their problem. Most people who are afraid of public speaking don't even consider that they have a phobia. They think it's normal to fear giving a wedding toast, reporting to a club, or appearing in court.

Only when the chips are down and they can no longer avoid public speaking do they go for help.

If you are one of the many who have this problem, recognize that your real fear is not of giving a speech. Rather, you are concerned that others will *perceive* that you are frightened while you speak. At a Phobia Society of America workshop, Dr. William L. Anixter, clinical director of the Roundhouse Square Psychiatric Center in Alexandria, Virginia, said that the fear of public speaking begins with *anticipatory anxiety*. Before you start to speak, you tell yourself you are afraid that you will not be able to speak, causing your anxiety level to rise. As you begin to speak, your expectations of failure bring on more nervousness. You see that all eyes are on you, and you fear that they will actually see that you feel shaky. Your expectations are fulfilled when your body calls in the fight-or-flight response, causing your legs to shake and your voice to choke up. You tell yourself that you are indeed making a fool of yourself, causing your body to send more adrenaline into your bloodstream. You are caught up in a vicious cycle of anticipatory anxiety, which leads to panic and nervousness, which leads to more panic.

In reality, said Dr. Anixter, the surge of adrenaline that causes you to shake and tremble has a very short half-life. If you can stop the fear thoughts that reinforce your anxiety for only a few minutes, you will be calm enough to speak well.

If you want to conquer your public speaking phobia, there are a wealth of tools you can use to start fooling your unconscious into sending you feelings of calm rather than anxiety. Here are some of them:

1. Join a support group in which you can desensitize yourself to your fear of speaking before a group. Toastmasters International is widely available. If your problem is so severe that this kind of lay help doesn't work, seek out a program such as the one at Roundhouse Square Psychiatric Center, where therapy, education, and practical experience in making speeches before others are combined.

(Roundhouse Square Psychiatric Center has an intensive weekend program that has helped people from across the country.)

2. Learn the techniques I employed to break the cycle of fear. These tools will enable you to function in the short period during which adrenaline is active in your body. These tools also prevent further adrenaline-producing thoughts. If you do not reinforce your anxiety, the adrenaline will dissipate quickly, and you will be calm for the remainder of the speech. Here are a few of these techniques:

- Slow down to what you may consider to be an abnormal rate of speaking during the time when you are experiencing fear symptoms. By slowing down, you give yourself a chance to breathe deeply, overcoming your tendency to freeze and not breathe at all. (Your audience will not perceive your slow speech as abnormal. You will simply appear to be speaking very deliberately and emphatically.) You can also use frequent pauses for the same purpose. Write them into the speech before you give it.

- Focus inward in a positive way. Before you give your speech, rate your fear on a scale of zero to ten. While speaking, tell yourself, "I'm experiencing a four" rather than "My legs are trembling and everyone will see."

- Focus outward by using your five senses to orient yourself to reality and the present moment rather than your fantasies of fear. Look at the room in which you are speaking and note the colors of the walls. Count the number of chairs, or notice details of light fixtures. Feel the wood in the podium, the carpet under your feet. Listen to the music coming from the next room or the sound of traffic outside. If your mind is busy with the delivery of the speech and with using the five senses, it cannot pay attention to fear.

- Choose one or two of these techniques, and write

down a cue word (such as *focus* or *slow*) to remind yourself to use them. Place your cues on your speech notes so that you will remember to use them.
Depend on self-education, not drugs. It is true that beta blockers like Tenormin or Inderol can enable you not to feel fear as you make a speech. However, if you are called on at work to make a sudden report, you won't have time to swallow a pill and then wait an hour while it takes effect. Recognize that you can get over your fear of public speaking without medications.

Your Goal Sheet for Overcoming Public Speaking Phobia

Here is how your goal sheet for getting over the fear of public speaking might look:

Long-Term Goal: On _____(date) I commit myself to overcoming my public speaking phobia.

Short-Term Goals:

1. I will investigate a support group in which I can make practice speeches and receive positive and constructive feedback.
2. I will join such a group and work to desensitize myself to my fear.
3. I will practice the tools that will enable me to break the public speaking fear cycle.
4. I will go to alpha three times a day and visualize and affirm that I enjoy public speaking.
5. I will restructure my *rejectionitis* thinking with cognitions of self-worth.
6. I will give myself "attaboys" or "attagirls" for every attempt to do public speaking, regardless of the consequences.

Don't forget to leave space on your goal sheet to check off whether you have worked on these goals every day.

FEAR-Smashing Shyness

Are you afraid to go alone to the movies, to a sports event, or to a meeting? Are you afraid to eat alone in a restaurant or go unaccompanied to a party, even when you are acquainted with the people who will be there? If so, you may have a fear that you don't think of as a phobia. You may simply be shy.

Shyness can be considered a social phobia, however, because when you are shy, you avoid persons or places because of your uncomfortable body sensations. Sweaty palms, blushing, feeling edgy—these are nothing more than low levels of anxiety that cause you to shrink from familiarity or contact with others. You get caught up into a fear cycle, because you continue to tell yourself that you *are* shy and that you *can't* participate in certain activities. Shyness can bring on a host of other social phobias.

You may not think of yourself as shy. I certainly never did. I was always perfectly comfortable in the presence of others. If I felt that all the attention was on me in a given situation, however, I had to use a lot of bluff to get through it. Until I found Life Plus and accepted myself for being who I was, I felt like a fraud in my relationships with others. I overcame these feelings by building my self-worth.

Peggy Arndt, a Los Angeles therapist who has helped many overcome their shyness, believes that some people are born with a temperament that makes them susceptible to becoming easily frightened and shy. If you had this temperament as a child, and a parent, teacher or other significant person heaped ridicule, criticism, or anger on you, you may become an adult who fears rejection. Each time you enter a situation or a place that has caused you shyness in the past, you replay in your mind the memories of former bad experiences, and your body sends you the appropriate anxious responses.

The good news, however, is that you can easily get over shyness. Arndt's therapy, based on the theories of neurolinguistic programming, often enables clients to overcome their shyness completely in only a few sessions. Since it is similar to the Emotional Transfusion process (FEAR-Smasher Number Three), I will describe it in detail. You will need a support person to do this.

1. Go to alpha and visualize a time when something wonderful happened to you and you felt outgoing rather than shy. It can be any experience that gives you the feeling you'd like to have when you are around other people. Perhaps you remember winning an award or sharing an intimate moment with a trusted loved one.

2. Play a movie of the entire scene in your mind. Don't try to see yourself. Simply be there, feeling the warmth or coolness of the air on your body, smelling the smells, seeing the beautiful colors, and hearing voices and sounds.

3. While you are enjoying this movie, have your support person anchor in this experience by touching your right forearm for thirty seconds.

4. Repeat this process, using a different happy scene, two more times, anchoring in the good feelings. Eventually you will be able to experience relaxed rather than anxious feelings in your body whenever the anchor is touched.

5. Now go into alpha, touch your anchor, and feel relaxed. Visualize a past experience in which you felt shy. Because you are in a relaxed, calm state, you will be able to watch the movie without feeling the anxiety that the experience originally caused. In this way you link calm body feelings neurologically with memories of shyness. You train your body to send you calm feelings whenever you think about entering a situation that used to cause shyness. You may want to do this a few times.

After using these techniques, your feelings of calm should continue even when you enter new situations that might cause shyness. To support this, you may want to go to alpha and visualize future situations that might cause shyness, seeing yourself reacting in an outgoing manner and being perfectly calm.

If this process does not work for you, consider the idea that you may not be willing to give up shyness because it is serving some positive role in their life. For instance, as a child, you may have protected yourself from the anger of others by being shy. As an adult, you continue to use shyness as a tool to avoid anger or confrontation. With professional counseling, you can learn more appropriate ways to relate to other people's anger. When you do, you will also be able to let go of your shyness.

The Shyness Goal Sheet

Here's how your goal sheet for overcoming shyness might look:

Long-Term Goal: On _____ (date) I will overcome shyness and enjoy being with other people.

Short-Term Goals:

1. I will practice Emotional Transfusion and anchoring to replace my body's fear sensations with feelings of calm.
2. I will write down my faulty cognitions about my self-worth and replace them with healthy affirmations.
3. I will desensitize myself to my shyness by seeking out ways I can relate to other people.

FEAR-Smashing School Phobia

Do your children have temper tantrums or sulk when you say they have to go to school? Do they have stomachaches, headaches, and sore throats that mysteriously disappear as soon as you let them stay home from school? If so, your children are like many others. They have school phobia.

In the spring-summer 1986 issue of the *Newsletter of the Phobia Society of America,* Dr. Richard Platt of FOCUS: A Private Mental Health Center in Albany, New York, said that school phobia may begin in the elementary grades because of a child's anxiety about separation from the mother. A more chronic form of school phobia starts in junior high and up.

Both types may begin after an unhappy incident in school, a brief illness, or enrollment in a new school. To overcome school phobia in your children, you should attempt to get them back into school as quickly as possible. You can use the same FEAR-Smasher keys you employ for your own phobias to help your children.

"A common error that parents and physicians alike make in their communication with the child is to reassure him or her that everything will be fine. Reassurance tends to increase the child's need for reassurance, only serving to strengthen the dependence and reinforce the fear," said Dr. Platt. He urged parents to solicit the help of the school and start gently with the smallest step the child will take in approaching or entering school.

When children complain of being afraid, the parents should say, "Of course you are afraid. Do this small step while feeling afraid." If you focus on the action you can take and not on how your child feels, you can avoid the mistake most parents make—paying attention to the anxiety and thus supporting its existence.

Here's what you can do:

1. Don't debate with your child whether or not he is really sick. If his temperature is under 100 degrees, he should at least approach the school. Ask your child's teacher to grant permission for him to go to the school nurse for thirty minutes or so if he feels faint or might vomit. Then have him return to class.

2. If your child resists all efforts, embark on a progressive desensitization plan. Solicit the help of the school. For a few days, your child may simply enter the school, have the office sign a note that he was there, and return home. Gradually your child can work up to going to class for a few minutes, then attending several classes, and finally going all day.

3. As your child takes each step, praise him for work well done.

4. If you cannot get your child back in school in roughly six weeks, seek professional assistance.

The Plain Truth About Social Phobias

There are multitudes of social phobias that I haven't mentioned from which you may suffer. However, as you can see by the ones I have detailed, getting over a social phobia is relatively easy, once you learn and use the tools that will help you. Whatever your phobia, make your goal sheet, work out your short-term goals, and practice desensitizing. Once you change your boss from Mr. Negative to Mr. Positive, you'll be out of the cage of your social phobia and free to enjoy your quest for Life Plus.

12

OVERCOMING LIFE-LIMITING FEARS

WHEN PEOPLE EXPRESS FLIGHT 14 from San Francisco to Newark was ready to go on May 26,1986, a wild-eyed man who "looked Iranian" suddenly bolted from his seat and ran out the door. Knocking aside startled security officers, he frantically tried to escape through locked doors in the terminal before an airport police officer tackled and subdued him. A terrorist? No. A very average American afraid to fly? Yes. Unfortunately, he was so frightened of being locked into the confines of the large Boeing 707 that he did the very thing he most feared: He made a fool of himself!

In fact, all 200 passengers were ordered off the plane; then all the baggage was removed. While police searched for a bomb and passengers fumed over the delay, the embarrassed man had to convince officials that he was simply afraid. He feared a mode of transportation used safely by thousands of people every day. Additional embarrassment came when his story was reported on national news programs and in virtually every newspaper in the country.

Why did this man let the mere thought of flying cause him to suffer such humiliation? He didn't understand it himself. He told investigators that he did not really expect the plane to crash. Nor was he panicky over the thought that the plane might be hijacked. He only knew that as he sat inside the airplane and heard the doors slam shut, he felt as if he were choking. His heart beat wildly. His mind flashed terrifying

147

pictures of the wings falling off, while he, locked in the tomblike interior, struggled helplessly to save himself. He was afraid he was going to faint or start shouting and screaming. Irrational fear just took over.

This man's experience is not unique. A Boeing Corporation study reports that one out of every ten people who fly on airlines is secretly (or not so secretly) afraid. Countless others won't fly at all. They avoid vacations that could be pleasurable, jeopardize advancement in business, and waste valuable time taking alternative modes of transportation, all because they "just can't fly."

Perhaps the phobia that limits the quality of your life is not that of flying but the fear of driving or of being in high places. If you can't operate your car, you are stranded in a society in which transportation by automobile is the accepted norm. If you are afraid to enter tall buildings, take an elevator, climb stairs, or cross a bridge, you can't function in today's world.

Avoiding planes, cars, tall buildings, elevators, stairs, and bridges is almost impossible in twentieth-century America. I call these fears the life-limiting phobias, because that's exactly what they are. Like people who have the social phobias described in Chapter 11, you can function with a life-limiting phobia—so long as you are willing to settle for second best. But you don't have to do that. Recovering from a life-limiting phobia can be relatively easy if you use the FEAR-Smasher keys.

My Experience with the Life-Limiting Phobias

I first became afraid to fly in the stressful year after my father died, before I had my first panic attack. One day as I sat in a departure lounge waiting for a plane, terror hit me without warning. I felt as if I were going to faint on the spot. I was not afraid of a crash. I just suddenly found myself thinking that I was going to be trapped in the plane, not ever able to get out. I had a terrible fear of losing control of my environment. Irrational, yes, but that fear made me miserable whenever I had to fly from then on until I found Life Plus.

I did not become fearful of driving until after I had my first panic attack. I would drive up to a red light and find that my hands were clenched on the steering wheel. I was gritting my teeth and fighting not to pass out. When I drove on an expressway, my feelings intensified. An exit sign to me was as welcome as a life preserver is to a sailor gone overboard.

Looking back, I know these fears could have been a result of the same three vulnerabilities that cause the social phobias I described in Chapter 11. I may have had a biological vulnerability that caused my fight-or-flight response trigger to be especially sensitive. I had the social vulnerability of worrying about what others thought about my less than perfect performance. And I had psychological vulnerability, too. I lacked the skills to cope with all the stress that was building up in my rain barrel and causing panic attacks.

My fears were completely *irrational*. You can also develop *rational* fear after a traumatic event, especially if you have the same three vulnerabilities. Perhaps a flight is bumpy, you're in a bad auto accident, or you get stuck in an elevator for several hours. Your unconscious begins to associate danger with these activities, which have never caused you fear in the past. The next time you have to fly, drive, or enter an elevator, your sensitized unconscious reminds you that the last time you did so, you had a bad experience. It signals your body to make your hands get sweaty and your breathing quicker.

If you haven't yet learned how to deal with such symptoms, you may begin to do "what if" thinking, which only reinforces this rational fear: "What if the engines of the plane fail? What if a drunk driver is in that car coming over the hill and loses control and hits me head on? What if this elevator breaks and falls all the way to the basement?" you may be thinking. If you "what if" long enough, all the while picturing the disastrous consequences in your mind, your unconscious feels that you really are crashing, hitting another car head on, or falling to the basement. Soon your unconscious is telling you, "No, you can't fly. You can't drive. You can't enter that elevator. It just isn't safe for you to do it, no matter what anyone says."

Finally, social vulnerability comes into play when you worry, "Others are going to see that I'm scared. They'll think I'm crazy." You've lost control and you don't like it. You may conclude that from then on, you had better avoid flying, driving, or riding in elevators. When you carry out that decision, you have a life-limiting phobia.

"That's just the way I am," you try to explain, playing the victim. But you really *don't* have to be that way! I firmly believe that with a little commitment and work, you can get over any life-limiting fear.

FEAR-Smashing the Fear of Flying

When she spoke at the Phobia Society of America's National Conference, Carol Cott Gross, director of the New York City Fear of Flying Course, related the amusing story of how her father, the late Nate Cott, originated the course. For thirty years, she said, Cott insisted on driving all the way from New York to Florida for the family's annual vacation. Friends teased him about the fact that he wouldn't fly. But Cott had all kinds of reasons.

"I just don't like being shut up in that toothpaste tube of an airplane cabin," he would tell his daughter. "Besides, nobody can give you a guarantee that the plane won't crash, and anyway, I like being able to see the same sights on the highway over and over." When his friends hinted that perhaps his IQ was none too high, he was determined to prove that intelligence had nothing to do with his irrational fear. In 1971, he placed a tiny classified ad in the *New York Times* stating, "If you're afraid to fly, call me." Hundreds responded, and when they did, he asked their IQ. Almost all of them were unusually intelligent.

But that wasn't the end of the story, because the people who responded were not in the mood for jokes. They begged Cott to organize "something like Alcoholics Anonymous for people who are afraid to fly." So Cott, a mechanical engineer by profession, found two psychologists who would cooperate with him and started just such a group.

That was the genesis of one of the first courses in the United States designed to help people overcome their fear of flying. Fifteen years later, even after his death, his course is still going strong.

If the fear of flying limits your life as it did for Nate Cott, realize that you can get over it. Many courses are now available throughout the country designed to help you overcome the biological, social, and psychological vulnerabilities that have caused your body to send in the fight-or-flight response at the very thought of flying. Some, like Cott's, function as ongoing support groups. In weekly meetings, you receive education by professionals in the airline industry, psychological counseling, and gradual exposure to flying. Others, like the fear-of-flying course taught by the Phobia Centers of the Southwest in Dallas, provide the same three-pronged approach condensed into the period of a single weekend. Either way, you will have the group support of other people like yourself as you desensitize yourself to your fears. You can learn together, fly together, and celebrate your successes together with a party at the end of the course. A whole new way of life will open up to you.

If you are afraid to fly, first try using my FEAR-Smasher keys. If you attempt to practice the keys with the aid of a good support person and still can't talk yourself into boarding a plane for flight, enroll in one of the fear-of-flying courses. Contact the major airlines for information on courses in your area. After you have discovered that you really can enjoy traveling by plane, you can use the FEAR-Smashers as a way of maintaining your freedom from fear.

Demystifying the Fear of Flying

Carol Cott Gross has been quoted as saying that people who are afraid to fly have one of two basic fears: that their panic symptoms will cause them to have a heart attack or stroke on the plane or that they will make a fool of themselves.

Neither of these fears has anything to do with the possibility that the plane will crash; however, strange noises on the plane, turbulence, or a newspaper account of a plane crash may cause you to experience the sweaty hands or faster heart rate of anticipatory anxiety. "What if" thoughts and gory fantasies may accelerate your symptoms. By adding inappropriate cognitions such as "With my luck, the plane will be hit by lightning" or "Other people are noticing that I look scared," you signal your aroused body to send in the adrenaline. The panic occurs, just as you told yourself it would.

The first step in breaking this vicious cycle is *education*. You need to know how planes fly, what all the strange noises are, and how safe it is to fly.

American Airlines captain Bill Evans, who teaches just this kind of information in the Phobia Centers of the Southwest's fear-of-flying course, likes to emphasize that flying is a good risk.

"A good businessman cannot reduce his financial risk to zero. Instead, he attempts to manage his risks by doing all he can to protect himself from prospects that seem dangerous. By using the same type of 'risk management' (not risk elimination), you can reduce your likelihood of being involved in an accident by choosing to participate in activities that are statistically safe," he tells his classes. "Only an average of 200 people die each year in accidents on major airlines in the United States. By contrast, 1500 die on farm vehicles or tractors, and 50,000 die in cars. The risk in flying is very low."

Here are seven of the worst worries about flying and new ways of thinking about them that will reduce your fear:

Worry Number One: If the plane's engines stop, the plane will nosedive.

Not true, says Evans, because the engines do not hold the plane in the air; the wings do. The curved design of the wing causes air to move faster across the top than across the bottom of the wing. The result is greater air pressure below, producing lift. Even a 500,000-pound 747 without power will glide from a height of 30,000 feet for 90 miles before coming to the ground. In fact, in order to make the plane descend, a pilot must at some point make a reduction in power for many minutes. The plane does not nosedive. It glides into a gentle descent to prepare for landing.

Worry Number Two: If flames shoot out of jet engines, they must be on fire.
Not true. Jet engines must burn large amounts of fuel to produce the hot gases that shoot out at high speed and propel the plane in flight. The flames are indications that engines are working properly.

Worry Number Three: A bumpy flight means that the pilot has lost control.
Not true. Bumpiness at low altitude is caused by sudden changes in the temperature of the air through which you travel. Warm air (usually found over cities and open fields) causes updrafts. Cool air (often found over woods and bodies of water) causes downdrafts. Turbulence can also be expected when flying through clouds. At high altitude, turbulence is caused when different air masses, including the fast-moving jet streams, collide with one another. These types of turbulence are normal (and safe). The turbulence found in thunderstorms *can* be dangerous, but radar instruments warn pilots of thunderstorms that would not be navigable. Standard safety procedure for all airline pilots is to detour thunderstorms.

Worry Number Four: When visibility is poor, the pilot cannot see well enough to land.
Not true. Radio navigation and special instruments can guide the plane down to the runway. In fact, some planes have automatic landing devices that are so sophisticated that they can locate runways through fog, clouds, and rain and then make the landing without any pilot input at all.

Worry Number Five: When it's too cold, ice is bound to cause the plane to crash.

Not true. Ice can cause crashes, but major airlines now have anti-icing and de-icing equipment on all planes that prevents the formation of ice.

Worry Number Six: Noises coming from the plane's engines or wings indicate that the plane is in trouble.
Probably not true. Noise can occur for many reasons—from the flaps going up to the landing gear being lowered to intentional changes in engine power settings. In a fear-of-flying course, you will have a chance to learn exactly what each noise means and why it is normal.

Worry Number Seven: Human error can't be ruled out.
True. Pilots *should* follow the safety regulations and detour around storms. They *should* turn de-icers on when they are needed. Pilots are human, and they can make mistakes just like everyone else. The risk of their doing so, however, is minimized by the stringent requirements of the FAA and major airlines for pilot training and experience. All airline aircraft are required to have at least two pilots in the cockpit. Each monitors the other to prevent pilot error. It is extremely unlikely that two (or more) pilots in the crew would make the same mistake at the same time. Remember, too, that these pilots are just as interested in arriving home safely as you are.

What You Can Do to Reduce the Fear of Flying

There are tools you can use to break the fear-of-flying cycle. To combat *anticipatory anxiety,* go to your secret resting place an hour before leaving for the airport. Because most people who fear flying have been in the habit of visualizing gory scenes of crashes, the temptation at alpha will be to let your mind picture the worst, not the best. Therefore, you might want to try visualizing a pleasant, restful scene with a lot of detail that prevents you from being distracted. Carol Cott Gross suggests a pleasant beach peopled with movie stars, an exciting game of tennis, or a gourmet dinner with all the visual and taste sensations.

At alpha you can also see yourself on the plane, enjoying talking to other people, and you can visualize the pleasant experiences you will have when you reach your destination.

As you visualize, affirm that you enjoy flying. Change your "what if" cognitions to such statements as "I have flown before and reached my destination safely" or "Millions of people fly safely every year, and so can I."

While on the plane, *reinforce calm feelings to your unconscious*. Here are some tricks for doing that:

- As you get on the plane, visit with the captain in the cockpit and tell him that you have been nervous about flying and are in the process of desensitizing yourself to your fear. You will find airline personnel sympathetic and helpful. As you talk to them, you will be impressed at the professionalism of the crew and the sophistication of the plane's equipment.
- If you feel nervous while waiting for the flight to begin, pretend you are a reporter who is assigned to write a story on the fact that people are afraid to fly. "Interview" other passengers about their feelings. If you find some who admit to being nervous, reassure them with the facts that you have learned about flying. By doing so, you will reinforce feelings of calmness in your own mind.
- If you are feeling tense while seated on the plane, practice relaxation procedures. Clench and release the muscles in your body, just as you do in the Alpha Script. Use the Calming Counts to breathe as you should.
- Wear a rubber band on your wrist, and snap it any time you notice that you are thinking anxiety-producing "what if" questions. Restructure these thoughts with positive affirmations about the safety of flying.
- Talk to your neighbor about the pleasant things you plan to do when you reach your destination. Ask about your neighbor's plans.

Your Goal Sheet for Breaking the Fear of Flying

Long-Term Goal: I commit myself to overcome my fear of flying.

Short-Term Goals:

1. I will read a book on aerodynamics so that I will understand how a plane flies.
2. I will go to alpha three times a day and visualize and affirm that I will enjoy flying.
3. I will write down the "what if" thoughts that come to my mind in one column and counter each one with rational cognitions, for example:

What If . . .	*Rational Cognition*
1. What if the flight gets bumpy and I am thrown up against the ceiling?	1. Even under very bumpy conditions, my seat belt will hold me securely in place.
2. What if the pilot is drunk and loses control?	2. The FAA requires that pilots not drink for eight hours before flights. The pilot is just as interested in safety as I am.

4. I will write out a hierarchy of fears about flying. I will then make a plan for desensitizing myself by following the progressive steps. I will refer to my fear feelings by number only.

5. I will find a support person.
6. I will work up to making an actual flight by first visiting an airport, then entering a departure lounge, then going inside a plane, and finally making a short flight. I will give myself "attaboys" or "attagirls" for every attempt I make, whether it is successful or not.
7. I will plan a pleasant destination for my first flight so that I will have something to look forward to.
8. I will visit the cockpit before I make a flight, interview others on the plane, and practice relaxation and cognitive restructuring while I am flying.
9. I will celebrate my successful flight.
10. If I try all these steps and still have a fear of flying, I will take a course in the fear of flying.

FEAR-Smashing the Driving Phobia

Amy wrote to tell me how happy she was that she had overcome her fear of driving. "One night I wanted to go to my friend's baby shower, but it was 20 miles away, and I would have had to drive across a bridge alone. I was terrified by the thought that I might have a panic attack and would be too far from a hospital to get there quickly," she told me. "I had to have my husband drive me to the party and come back for me. I'm glad I don't have to make him do things like that anymore."

Amy's driving phobia was due to the panic attacks that also occurred when she was in crowded places.

Charles's driving phobia began a different way. After he was injured in an auto accident twenty years ago, he was afraid to take the wheel of his car.

Margo's reason for not driving on busy streets was that she felt other drivers were pushing her to go faster than she would like. It didn't occur to her that as long as she followed the law, she had the right to drive at the rate she wanted.

Phil wouldn't drive at all. When he got behind the wheel, he had strange impulses to aim his car directly at a pedestrian.

All four had different reasons why they developed a phobia about driving. Phil needed professional counseling to get over his phobia. Amy, Charles, and Margo learned to desensitize themselves to their fear by using good support persons and the FEAR-Smasher keys.

The "Why Am I Afraid to Drive?" Quiz

Answer the questions to determine the underlying reason for your fear of driving.

1. Do you remember a traumatic event that marked the beginning of your fear about driving? Many people drive without fear until they are in an automobile accident or have other scary experiences such as being on a roller coaster. If you answered yes to this question, your unconscious has become sensitized to the fear caused by the traumatic event. You may also have the biological vulnerability that causes you to experience fear symptoms more easily than normal people. You can get over this fear by desensitizing yourself.

2. If you cannot remember a traumatic event that was the beginning of your fear, ask yourself whether you have spontaneous panic attacks at other times than when you are driving. If so, you need to practice the relaxation and cognitive restructuring keys that will enable you to overcome panic attacks. After you are having some success, desensitize yourself to your driving phobia.

3. Do you have any hidden reasons for not driving that you don't quite admit even to yourself? If you answer yes to this question, you may need professional counseling in order to drive again. Therapists know that some clients unconsciously develop a driving phobia as a way of saying no—perhaps to an offer of a job that they really don't want to take that requires driving. They may refuse to drive as a way of accommodating a controlling family member who doesn't want to be separated from them or of rebelling against a family member whom they really don't want to drive to visit. With the help of a counselor,

you can learn to be assertive and communicate your needs rather than try to solve or avoid problems by not driving.

4. Do you refuse to drive because you tell yourself you don't care whether you ever go anywhere? Sometimes people who have a driving phobia become depressed and self-critical because they feel that something is seriously wrong with them. If this is your problem, just learning that you are not crazy and that you can recover from this phobia may free you to want to take action. You can desensitize yourself to your fear of driving.

5. Are you afraid to drive because you feel you don't drive well enough to avoid accidents? If you answered yes, signing up for a course with a good driving school may be the answer. It is rational to fear driving if you lack the skills to drive safely. If you commit yourself to learn, you can do so.

What You Can Do to Reduce the Fear of Driving

Here are some things you can do to overcome your phobia of driving regardless of the reason you have it:

1. In your notebook, write your five greatest fears about driving in one column, and counter them with rational affirmations, for example:

My Fears	*Affirmations*
1. Whenever I sit in the driver's seat of the car, I am afraid I will hyperventilate.	1. I am dealing with driving panic, and I know what to do. I can practice relaxation and the Calming Counts, and the fear will go away.

| 2. I am afraid that other drivers who tailgate will force me to drive too fast and I will have an accident. | 2. I am a worthy person, and I don't have to be pushed around by anyone. I can drive at any legal speed I desire. |

2. Write out your hierarchy of fears and fear sensations. Refer to your fear sensations by number from then on.

3. Go to alpha several times a day, especially before you are going to drive. Visualize yourself driving wherever you want, having a good time. If you feel fear sensations while you are at alpha, visualize that you are turning down a dial that measures the amount of fear you feel. Use Emotional Transfusion to replace fear sensations with happy thoughts. While at alpha, affirm that you are feeling relaxed and in control.

4. If you are agoraphobic, transfer your safe place from your home to your auto by decorating the car's interior with homey things like photos of your children, slogans, and smile stickers. Bring along refreshments that you can enjoy in your car.

5. With the help of a support person, begin desensitizing yourself to your fear. If necessary, spend some time just sitting in the car watching traffic pass while you practice relaxation techniques. Progress to driving slowly over traffic-free roads with your support person. After you are driving comfortably there, move on to highways and busy city streets. If you are afraid to go beyond certain boundaries, gradually extend the distance you will drive away from home. Eventually, start driving without your support person.

6. Give yourself the freedom to do whatever you must do to drive safely. If you can drive no faster than 30 miles per

hour (and the legal limit allows you to drive at that speed), affirm that it is perfectly all right for you to do so, even if you think that others expect you to drive faster.

7. To reduce edgy feelings while driving, breathe deeply, sing, or play the car radio. Talk to the truckers over your CB and tell them about your driving phobia. They will likely express their willingness to help you if you need it.

8. Wear a rubber band around your wrist, and if you begin to feel nervous, snap it. If you feel your panic beginning to rise, slow down, put on your flashing lights, and, if you need to, drive off onto the shoulder to give yourself time to calm down. If you feel like crying, that's OK, too. After you are calm again, you can drive some more.

9. Regardless of the outcome of each attempt to drive, give yourself an "attaboy" or "attagirl" for trying.

Your Goal Sheet for Getting Over the Fear of Driving

Long-Term Goal: On _____(date) I commit myself to getting over my fear of driving.

Short-Term Goals:

1. I will write down my thoughts about driving and determine the cause of my fears. If I need counseling, I will seek it.

2. I will write out my hierarchy of fears.

3. I will go to alpha three times a day and visualize and affirm that I enjoy driving and that I am a worthy person who deserves to drive in the way that I want.

4. I will begin desensitizing myself to my fear of driving with the help of a support person.

5. I will keep a journal of my progress and give myself "attaboys" or "attagirls" for every attempt to drive.

FEAR-Smashing the Fear of Heights

"Fain would I climb, yet fear I to fall," once wrote Sir Walter Raleigh, the seventeenth-century English adventurer and colonizer of the New World. His patroness, Queen Elizabeth, is reported to have written underneath Raleigh's words, "If thy heart fails thee, climb not at all."

Of such well-meaning advice are phobias made. We are all born with the fear of falling. In fact, this instinct protects us from the danger of smashing ourselves to pieces from the time we are toddlers until we are hobbling around on canes. It is rational to fear falling. It is, however, irrational to panic in high places like tall buildings, solidly anchored bridges, stairs with handrails, and well-functioning elevators. If you have such an irrational fear and you avoid those places, you have *acrophobia*, a fear of heights.

Psychiatrist Dr. Manuel Zane reports just how irrational this fear is in the book *Your Phobia*. He tells of a tree-trimmer who hangs from the top of 75-foot-high trees by only the cleats in his boots and a belt yet experiences a panic attack when looking out the window of an office building.

If you have the biological, social, and psychological vulnerabilities, it is easy for your unconscious to become overly sensitized to the normal fear of heights. You may stand at an observation deck overlooking a city street below and feel slightly dizzy. Then your imagination runs wild with visualizations of what would happen to you if you fell over the edge. Perhaps you almost feel a compulsion to throw yourself off. Your sensitive unconscious receives the danger signal and triggers your brain's fight-or-flight response. Once you experience the bodily sensations of fear, you slip into a downward spiral of anxiety, frightened thoughts, and more body sensations.

The list of high places you can fear is almost endless. Ladders, escalators, bridges—anything from which you can look down and imagine yourself falling can bring on the fight-or-flight response once you are sensitized to heights.

At the very worst, you may even fear the interiors of high

buildings even though you can't see anything but four walls and a floor. You may fear an elevator, not only because it is a closed-in space that causes you to sense the loss of control but also because you know it is taking you to an upper floor.

If you are acrophobic, you may avoid going to office buildings, theaters, and coliseums. You may even fear visiting a friend whom you have to drive over a bridge to reach. Acrophobia is truly a life-limiting phobia.

How You Can Get Over Your Fear of Heights

Here's how you can use the FEAR-Smashing keys to get over your fear of heights:

1. Prepare for desensitizing yourself by writing out your hierarchy of fear symptoms and referring to your fears by number rather than symptom.

2. Change your cognitions about heights. Write down your irrational fears and counter them with the facts. Here is an example:

My Fears	*The Facts*
1. I cannot approach a tall building without having feelings of panic.	1. I can use the FEAR-Smasher keys to reduce my anxiety.
2. It is unsafe for me to look out the window of a tall building because I might have a heart attack.	2. I know how to deal with panic. Fear symptoms are not dangerous and will pass if I think positive thoughts.

3. Go to alpha and visualize yourself being perfectly relaxed and smiling as you approach a tall building, then enter it, and finally go to the observation deck and look

down into the street below. Visualize a similar gradual desensitization to any other high place that you fear.

4. With the help of a support person, go to a high building. Walk up one flight of stairs together and look out the window. Then let your support person walk up the next flight of stairs and you follow. Keep going all the way to the top.

5. Use deep breathing, muscle relaxation, and Calming Counts if you feel anxiety while desensitizing.

6. Let your support person help you, but don't depend on him or her for everything. It's OK to hold on to your support person when you approach a railing if you are frightened. Have your support person remind you to look around at your surroundings rather than "freezing" and staring at a fixed object and to compliment you for every attempt you make.

7. If you have to retreat while you are feeling panic, that is OK. Calm yourself and then continue exposure to high places.

8. Reassure yourself of the safety of the high places you visit. As you approach a bridge, stop and ask the person in the toll booth any questions you might have about the safety of the bridge. Ask if there is a person available to drive you over or to come to your aid if you experience panic and have to stop.

9. Always give yourself "attaboys" or "attagirls" for any attempts to desensitize, whether successful or not.

Your Goal Sheet for Getting Over the Fear of Heights

Long-Term Goal: On _____ (date) I commit myself to get over my fear of heights.

Short-Term Goals:

1. I will write out my hierarchy of fears about heights and refer to my fear symptoms by number only.

2. I will go to alpha three times a day and visualize myself going to high places feeling perfectly relaxed and calm. I will affirm that I enjoy going to these high places.

3. I will act *as if* by gradually desensitizing myself to the high places that I fear, using a support person if necessary.

4. I will keep a journal of my progress, giving myself "attaboys" or "attagirls" for every attempt I make to recover from my acrophobia.

FEAR-Smashing the Urban Fears

If you are afraid of being in an enclosed space, such as a bathroom with locked doors or an elevator, you have *claustrophobia*, a very common fear. You can't bear the irrational thought that you might never get out. Even when you know that you can pound on the door and attract someone who will release you, the mere idea of being trapped brings on physical symptoms of anxiety. Then you have another worry: Other people will *see* that you are frightened! This anticipatory anxiety adds to your fear. Before you know it, you are avoiding any place where you will be enclosed.

When you live in a city, it is virtually impossible to avoid claustrophobic situations. These may seem even more frightening if the noise and jostling of crowds cause you to feel that you are being pressed in or confined. There is just no way you can function in a bustling metropolis without using subways, buses, and elevators and going to places like crowded malls, concerts, and movie theaters (where darkness adds another component of fear). That is why I call these life-limiting phobias the "urban fears."

As with the other fears I have listed in this chapter, you don't have to play the victim and miss out on the excitement and fun of living in a city. Use FEAR-Smasher Number One, take responsibility for your irrational urban fears, and set your goals for overcoming them.

What You Can Do to Reduce Urban Fears

Here is how you can use the other FEAR-Smasher keys to get over your fears of claustrophobia and crowds:

1. Prepare to desensitize yourself by writing out your hierarchy of fear symptoms and referring to a number rather than specific symptoms.

2. Write down your irrational fears and counter them with the facts. Here is an example.

My Fears	*The Facts*
1. The power will fail, and I will be trapped in an elevator.	1. The power is not likely to fail. If it does, I can use the emergency phone or pound on the door, and someone will come and let me out.
2. If I get on a bus, I might have a panic attack, and then other people will see how afraid I am.	2. If I have a panic attack on a bus, I can use Calming Counts and focusing techniques to gain control. I can also give myself permission to get off the bus at the next stop.

3. Go to alpha and visualize yourself as enjoying being in an elevator, a crowded mall, a theater, or a subway.

Affirm that you enjoy going places in the city and that you feel perfectly calm.

4. Talk to your support person about the worst thing that could happen to you if you went to the place you fear. Then go with your support person and check out safety features. For instance, check out the inspection report posted in the elevator, and note the last date on it. See if the emergency telephone works. Note exits in theaters and malls. Check out fire extinguishers and emergency stairways in subway tunnels.

5. Desensitize with your support person by gradually approaching the place that causes you the *least* amount of fear, then going on to enter it, and then to staying in it alone. For instance, if you are least afraid of traveling by bus, go with your support person during the period of the lowest ridership, get on the bus, sit side by side, and ride a few blocks before getting off. Gradually increase the distance you ride; then ride with your partner sitting several seats behind you. Finally progress to riding alone. Once you have mastered your least feared situation, you will find it easier to risk desensitizing yourself to one that holds more fear, such as the subway.

6. Use focusing techniques to reduce feelings of panic. Focus outward by counting the tiles on the floor, reading the ads in the subway, or describing the clothes that someone else is wearing. Wear a rubber band and snap it when you feel anxiety coming on; then affirm to yourself that you are feeling calm, that you love yourself and deserve to be calm.

7. Talk to other people to distract yourself. Reach out ot others and be helpful to them.

8. Talk to your panic. Tell it to go away. Carry affirmations in your billfold. If you feel nervous, take them out and read them.

9. Wear low-heeled shoes so that you can feel the ground under your feet and walk safely. Move around frequently in theaters and malls.

10. Always give yourself "attaboys" or "attagirls" for any attempts to desensitize, whether successful or not.

Your Goal Sheet for Getting Over Urban Fears

Long-Term Goal: On _____ (date) I commit myself to get over my fear of _____.

Short-Term Goals:

1. I will write out my hierarchy of fears about the situation that makes me least afraid and refer to my fear symptoms by number only.
2. I will go to alpha three times a day and visualize myself going into this situation feeling perfectly relaxed and calm. I will affirm that I enjoy going there.
3. With the help of my support person, I will gradually desensitize myself to this situation.
4. I will give myself "attaboys" or "attagirls" for every attempt I make to stay in this situation.
5. When I have mastered the situation that causes the least amount of dread, I will work on a new goal of getting over a situation that causes me more fear.

The Joy of Overcoming Life-Limiting Phobias

If you have ever cast a wistful eye at someone you know who seems absolutely fearless, able to go wherever he or she wants and to enjoy whatever pleasures life presents, stop wasting your time. When you start using the FEAR-Smasher keys to overcome your life-limiting phobias, you can be that very person. Don't wait. Take responsibility for yourself; do just one thing *today* to take charge of your fears, and you will be on the road to recovery.

13

SAYING GOODBYE TO THE SINGLE PHOBIAS

M Y FRIEND KURT had a cat phobia. An excellent sales-
man who never flinched while making a cold call
on the most prestigious prospect, he couldn't bring
himself to stay in the same room with a gentle tabby.

"I just can't bear being around cats. Their eyes staring at
me and their fur make my skin crawl. It's the way they can
jump at you. It's—well, I know it's irrational, but that's just
the way I feel, so I avoid any place where cats will be," he told
me.

Kurt is not alone. No one has even tried to tabulate the
number of people who have *ailourophobia*, an irrational fear
of cats. Most who have this phobia simply avoid cats, just as
Kurt did.

Then one day Kurt found that his strategy of avoiding cats
no longer worked. He was in love with a woman named
Shirley, whose pet Persian, Sascha, had been her most significant other for years. He wanted to marry Shirley, but what
could he do? He was terrified of entering Shirley's apartment
while Sascha was there. And Shirley had laid down the ul-
timatum, "Take me with Sascha or not at all."

When Kurt came to me, I told him about the FEAR-
Smasher keys. Within a very short time, Kurt was over his cat
phobia, and I was invited to a wedding.

That's the good news about cat phobia and every other kind of phobia that stems from one stimulus alone. If you have what Jim Wilson and other phobia therapists call a single phobia, you can say goodbye to it by practicing my FEAR-Smasher keys until it goes away. You *can* get over single phobias.

The list of stimuli that cause some people to run at so much as even a picture includes animals, birds, snakes, and insects; natural elements such as snow, thunder, or lightning; biological components such as blood or other people's eyes; and objects such as knives or scissors. You could be phobic of practically anything. As long as you have only one fear, your path to recovery should be relatively easy. According to a report by Dr. James Reich of the Department of Psychiatry of the University of Iowa College of Medicine in the March 1986 *Journal of Nervous and Mental Disease,* single phobias like these respond best to behavioral treatment. Some even have the potential of spontaneous remission. In children who have them, even highly disruptive single phobias tend to resolve without long-term negative consequences.

But you may not be willing to wait for a spontaneous remission. Like Kurt, you may suddenly find that your innocuous little phobia is presenting some big problems. If so, do as Kurt did and start using the FEAR-Smashers. First Kurt took responsibility for his own recovery by setting his goal and taking action. He asked Shirley to be his support person and help him desensitize himself to his fear of cats. Shirley agreed, and together they worked out a step-by-step plan. First, in Kurt's apartment, they looked together at pictures of cats. When he could do that without being overwhelmed by the terrible fear that cats always gave him, they went to Shirley's apartment and stood at the front door and talked. After Kurt could do that without feeling too much anxiety, they entered her apartment and talked while Sascha was locked in the bathroom. The next step was to sit in the same room, then to approach Sascha, and finally to pet her. Eventually Kurt was able to hold Sascha in his lap, even when Shirley was not in the room.

Kurt found that by using FEAR-Smasher Number Three—going to alpha and seeing himself in a calm, happy mood with Sascha—he could reduce his fears when he actually did approach the cat. He made use of Emotional Transfusion by holding on to all the good feelings he had when he visualized himself with Shirley while he substituted a visualization of himself with Shirley's cat.

Why You Have a Single Phobia

The phobia you have may be triggered by a single stimulus but may have many causes. Here are some of the ways in which you could have become sensitized.

Your parents may have modeled fearful behavior. Did your mother cower whenever she heard thunder during a spring storm? If so, you grew up believing that this harmless element of nature was dangerous. Much as you learned from your parents that laughter was appropriate at a party, you learned that the emotion of fear was "appropriate" during a storm. If this is your problem, you can easily desensitize yourself to your fear.

Your fear of an object that really does hold potential danger may have escalated because of a bad experience. Nearly all of us have instinctive fears of snakes and insects that sting (and most of our parents have, too!). However, the healthy fear that makes you wary of insects and snakes can become an anxiety-generating phobia that causes you to flee when others would stay, once you become sensitized. You may have been badly stung by a wasp, for instance, or a bully may have threatened you with a harmless snake that he told you was poisonous. You don't know quite what to do with this fear, so you begin to avoid snakes. The same thing happens with any pet that can scratch, bite, or peck when aroused. If this is the cause of your phobia, you can desensitize by using the FEAR-Smashers.

You may unconsciously associate an object with something else that you feel is dangerous. For instance, you may faint at the sight of blood because you associate it with killing or with death. If you have seen a gory accident, you might associate the horror of that moment with the blood that you saw spilled there. You sent yourself the message "Blood is dangerous." The result was that you developed a habit of feeling fear whenever you saw blood. Desensitization will help you overcome the fear habit.

A more complicated form of this kind of phobia is posttraumatic stress disorder. PTSD, as it is called, is not really a single phobia. It stems from such trauma as fighting in a bloody war, being raped or attacked, being abused as a child, undergoing disfiguring surgery, or witnessing a violent crime or accident. If you have had such a terrifying experience, you may suffer flashbacks, panic, or nightmares even years later whenever something happens to remind you of the original trauma. PTSD may cause you to feel overcome with guilt and depression. You can recover from PTSD by reliving the fear-producing events in the presence of other victims who understand and can demonstrate that they care, or with a therapist.

Freud's explanation of why people develop phobias is that they cannot cope with the unacceptable sexual or aggressive wishes they have as children. For instance, a 5-year-old, while going through the oedipal phase of development, may unconsciously wish to kill his father to take his place as his mother's sexual partner. Rather than carrying out these universal urges (which some people feel more strongly than others), the child represses them. Repression, however, creates anxiety, which becomes so painful that he makes use of a defense mechanism known as displacement: He substitutes the acceptable fear of a harmless object, such as fire, running water, or a fly, for the unacceptable fear of killing his father. By using displacement, he can maintain control of his fear by simply avoiding fire, running water, or a fly. When he becomes an adult, however, with the repressed urges buried in his unconscious, he cannot understand why fire, running water, or a fly causes him anxiety.

Freud's explanation used to be the standard one for all phobias and the rationale for treating patients with lengthy psychoanalysis. Today many psychiatrists recognize that behavioral methods of treatment suffice for single phobias.

However, if behavioral methods do not work, psychoanalytic treatment may be in order.

It is also possible that you may be using a phobia to resolve a conflict in your life. In his compelling book *Don't Panic*, Dr. R. Reid Wilson, a psychologist and the director of the Clinical Hypnosis Training Program at the Southeast Institute in Chapel Hill, North Carolina, reports the case of a woman who developed a fear of knives in this way. She believed that her phobia began when she found her 7-year-old son threatening his sister with a kitchen knife. After dwelling on the dangers of knives with her son, she herself began to fear her ability to control a knife, so she avoided knives. While in therapy, however, the real reason for the phobia surfaced. She was in an unstable marriage and wanted to have another baby. She felt she needed more support from her husband during the pregnancy but was afraid to ask for it for fear that he would decide the marriage was unworkable and ask for a divorce. By developing the fear of knives, she could tell herself that she wasn't capable enough to run her household and therefore should not have another child. She resolved her internal conflict and also avoided confronting the pain in her marriage. If your phobia is an attempt to solve internal conflict, therapy will help you.

You may develop a single phobia as a result of having other phobias. For instance, if you are agoraphobic, you may fear leaving your safe place, but your anxiety may cause you also to develop a fear of water. Nita wrote to tell me that her panic attacks kept getting worse and worse. She could no longer drive on a busy street, nor could she go anywhere far from home if her children weren't with her. She was fast on the way to becoming housebound. Nita was so anxious about everything that she began to displace her fear on other things as well. For no explainable reason, she developed a fear of water. She couldn't wash her hair because she was terrified at having her head under water. She even feared drinking cold water, because she felt that it would take her breath away from her, much as her panic attacks did.

I advised Nita to work on her agoraphobia first. Once she

desensitized herself to her fear of going out of the house, she could then make a goal sheet to overcome her fear of water.

Using the FEAR-Smashers to Overcome Single Phobias

Getting over a single phobia is like overcoming a bad habit. You replace your old ways of doing things with new ways and practice them until they feel right. You train your unconscious to respond automatically in the way you want it to. FEAR-Smasher Number Four (risk developing your ability to attempt new things) is the most important key in overcoming a single phobia. You can risk getting a support person, making a plan for desensitizing, and then actually going out and following the plan. Here are some tips for making desensitization easier:

- Plan to desensitize by small steps. Don't jump from looking at pictures of snakes to handling them. Plan intermediate steps, such as talking about snakes, going to the zoo, and approaching the herpetarium before you enter it. And, yes, it's OK to stop short of *handling* snakes. If you can be calm while in their presence, that's probably enough!
- Set up a schedule when you will work on exposure, and hold to it. Practice at least two or three times a week.
- Don't expect to be completely free of fear before moving on to the next step. When you feel fear, describe it to your support person by number according to your hierarchy of fears (see Chapter 8) rather than by symptom. Focus outward and affirm to yourself that you are in control and that the fear will pass.
- Prepare ahead of time by changing your cognitions about your fear. Are you making excuses about why it's impossible for you to come in contact with the feared object? If so, you are thinking in *stretch-or-shrink* terms. Remind yourself that you are not a victim and that you can use the tools that will make it possible for you to desensitize.
- Go to alpha and see yourself responding to your feared stimulus in a perfectly calm manner. Make an Image Book

to enhance your visualizations (see Chapter 15). Write affirmations such as "Whenever I am around insects, I feel perfectly calm." Anchor in good feelings to go with your visualizations (see Chapter 7).

- Be gentle to yourself, even when you have to retreat. Refuse the temptation of telling yourself, "I *should* or *ought* to be doing better than I am." Affirm that you are a person of worth, even if you're not perfect. Give yourself "attaboys" or "attagirls" for every attempt you make.
- Celebrate your successes. Each time you are able to go a step farther, reward yourself. Buy something extravagant if your budget permits, or allow yourself to take a bubble bath or to sleep an extra half hour on Saturday. Tell yourself how proud you are of yourself in your journal.

Your Goal Sheet for Getting Rid of a Single Phobia

Long-Term Goal: On _____ (date) I commit myself to conquer my fear of _____.

Short-Term Goals:

1. I will write down five negative feelings I have about practicing desensitization and counter each one with rational statements.

2. I will go to alpha three times a day and visualize and affirm that I am perfectly relaxed when I am around _____ (my feared object). If I have difficulty in visualizing, I will make an Image Book (Chapter 15). If I feel nervous while visualizing my feared stimulus, I will use Emotional Transfusion (see Chapter 7).

3. I will ask someone to be my support person and have him or her read this book in order to help me.

4. I will set up a schedule for desensitizing, and I will reward myself each time I work on desensitizing with an "attaboy" or "attagirl" *regardless* of the outcome.

5. I will celebrate my successes by _____.

14

THE GIFT
OF AGORAPHOBIA

I N *JONATHAN LIVINGSTON SEAGULL,* Richard Bach says there is no problem you receive in life that does not have a gift in its hands. To an audience of agoraphobics, I say the same thing in a different way. "Agoraphobia is the best thing that ever happened to me," I tell them. If you are agoraphobic and you think that sounds crazy, I understand. When my agoraphobia was causing me to have a panic attack every time I stepped outside the front door to pick up my newspaper, I certainly didn't see this disorder as a gift. I couldn't go anywhere—not to the movies, not to a restaurant, not even to the supermarket—without my heart beating so hard that I thought I was dying. I would feel faint, disoriented, and terrified. I was sure I was going to lose control and start shouting obscenities in public. How could anything that caused me so much misery be the best thing that ever happened to me?

Here's why it was. To get over my agoraphobia, I had to learn the tools that would permit me to understand myself, to accept myself, and to grow. I had to commit myself to using the tools. When I did use them, I mastered them. Then I knew once and for all that no irrational fear could ever have any power over me anymore. My agoraphobia was gone, and now I had the courage to deal with any other problem in my life. I had the potential for achieving great things no matter what happened to me. Had agoraphobia not made me so miserable, I never would have had the desperate incentive to learn the techniques that would later bring me Life Plus.

If you don't see agoraphobia as a gift, you may be like so many people who write or phone me. They *want* to reprogram and desensitize themselves, but they tell themselves they *can't* because they are just too scared. They are stuck with an irrational fear of the symptoms.

Gwen wrote to tell me that she was engaged to a wonderful man but she was afraid she would never be married. She was just too afraid that she would have panic attacks. First of all, she was certrain that she would have a panic attack during the wedding ceremony. And if she had to move to a new apartment, she was afraid that she would suffer constantly from the tension headaches, the light-headedness, and the fear she was going to faint or lose control that plagued her whenever she left her own home. For four pages of her letter, she described the terrible sensations she so dreaded. Then she ended with, "No doctor has ever been able to do anything to help me, not even with medication. I've tried cognitive restructuring and relaxation, but they just don't work for me. What more can I do?"

I know from personal experience how hard it is to go through the terrifying feelings that Gwen is having. I know the temptation to dwell on symptoms by writing page after page in a journal or by talking about them constantly. How much easier it is to throw up your hands and tell yourself you are a hopeless case than to make a commitment to help yourself and then do it. How much simpler just to stop going anywhere or doing anything with anyone outside of your home. You tell yourself you're a victim, and there's nothing you can do about it.

If this is your problem, take the first step that will lead you to your gift. Use the first FEAR-Smasher and take responsibility for your agoraphobia. You are not a victim, and you *can* do something about it.

Using the First FEAR-Smasher:
What Do You Know About Agoraphobia?

If you are to use the FEAR-Smashers to overcome agoraphobia, it is essential that you have a basic understanding of what this disorder really is. Evaluate the following statements as either true or false to see how much you know about agoraphobia. Then use the first FEAR-Smasher and commit yourself to learning everything you can about it.

1. My agoraphobia is a symptom of mental instability and will make me insane.

False. Agoraphobia is the condition of having such an overwhelming fear of having a panic attack that you avoid going anywhere where you believe you will have an attack. Many agoraphobics become so afraid of panic attacks that they avoid all places and activities except their "safe place," usually their home. Although phobias are a psychiatric disorder, they do not make you mentally ill.

2. I must have something terribly wrong with me if I have agoraphobia.

You don't have something terribly wrong, but you likely have three vulnerabilities—psychological, biological, and social. When you are unable to cope with stress because of your *psychological* vulnerability, your anxiety level begins to build. Your *biological* vulnerability adds to your problems. Your overly sensitive body interprets your high level of stress as danger and tries to protect you by producing large quantities of adrenaline, which causes the fight-or-flight response. The physical effects, in the absence of real danger, are uncomfortable and frightening. Because of your *social* vulnerability, you tell yourself that others will see that you are afraid and ridicule you, or you think that something must be terribly wrong with you. This kind of self-talk increases your anxiety, reinforcing the likelihood of having more panic attacks.

*3. I could die from the symptoms of panic attack: a racing
heart, choking sensations, or hyperventilation.*

False. These fight-or-flight symptoms are the very ones you
would experience in a situation that actually is dangerous,
such as meeting up with a bear or finding yourself in a burning house. These bodily changes enable you to fight or run
with greater strength than you could in your usual state.
Since these changes are entirely normal, they cannot be dangerous to you, unless you have an underlying physical condition that would be exacerbated by them. A thorough evalua-
tion by your physician can tell you whether or not this might
be a factor.

*4. If I have too much stress, there's nothing I can do to
prevent sicknesses like migraine headaches, low back pain,
stomach ulcers, or panic attacks.*

False. A buildup of stress can trigger the symptoms of
psychosomatic illnesses or panic attacks. If you learn how to
use psychological, physical, and nutritional tools to cope with
stress, however, you don't have to have either condition. By
learning to call in Mr. Positive, change harmful self-talk about
yourself into rational thoughts, and accept your self-esteem,
you can use your mind to signal your body not to send you a
fight-or-flight response. You do not have to have panic attacks,
no matter how stressful your life is. After I learned these
coping skills to overcome my agoraphobia, I was completely
free of panic attacks, even though I underwent the stress of a
divorce, a mid-life crisis, a new career, and having to appear
on national TV shows.

*5. Once I have been sensitized to a certain situation by irra-
tional fear, my body tends to react to that situation with symptoms and possibly a panic attack every time I confront it.*

True. Panic attacks are like bad habits. They keep recurring
unless we do something to overcome the bad habit. By gradually exposing ourselves to situations outside of our safe place,
we can desensitize ourself—reverse our body's bad habit of
producing the fight-or-flight response at inappropriate times.

6. *If I am away from my safe place and have a panic attack, I can use special techniques to make the panic go away.*

True. With focusing techniques, affirmations, Calming Counts, and the realization that the panic attack is not dangerous, you can stay in the situation and the panic will subside as the effect of the adrenaline in your bloodstream wears off.

7. *If I take medication that blocks my panic, I don't need to learn to use such tools.*

False. Even doctors who recommend medication do not believe that you should continue taking it indefinitely. If you do not learn these tools, there is a high likelihood of relapse after you stop taking the medication.

8. *Few people ever get over agoraphobia.*

False. Countless numbers of people, myself included, have recovered from agoraphobia by using the five FEAR-Smasher keys. Give yourself a chance to recover. Risk trying new things to help yourself, and the rewards will be great.

9. *Using the FEAR-Smashers is hard to do.*

That depends. The FEAR-Smashers are simple but not easy. They work, but they require persistence. But they offer so many other rewards in personal growth that you may look at them as an adventure that in itself becomes enjoyable. You are worth the effort you will have to expend. You are a special person with many gifts, and once you have overcome agoraphobia, you will have an even greater gift—the ability to help others overcome agoraphobia.

10. *I can use the first FEAR-Smasher to start overcoming my agoraphobia today.*

True. Stop playing the victim. Take responsibility for getting over agoraphobia by setting your long-term goal to recover completely. I will show you how to use the other FEAR-Smashers to help you overcome your biological, psychological, and social vulnerabilities. In Chapter 15 you wil find many practical tips that will make it easier to use the keys.

The Second FEAR-Smasher:
Developing Your Self-worth

Before I learned to use the tools that helped me conquer agoraphobia, my image of myself was that of a loser. Never mind that I was a successful businessman. Whenever I talked to myself about myself, I was the person who could never do things as well as other people. I focused on my inabilities and constantly berated myself for not being better than I was. No wonder my unconscious sent me anxious feelings. I was under fire—from myself.

That is why my second FEAR-Smasher is "Establish your self-worth." If you are agoraphobic, you need to call in Mr. Positive and start thinking good things about yourself. You can do this through cognitive restructuring and nurturing the little child inside of you (see Chapter 6). Also, use the many practical ideas in Chapter 15 for enhancing your self-image.

The Third FEAR-Smasher:
Reprogramming at Alpha

When I was housebound with agoraphobia, I had plenty of time on my hands, and I used it to my advantage by going to alpha six times a day. Sometimes I went to my secret resting place and just stayed there, enjoying the calm and peace that it brought. At other times I reprogrammed myself with visualizations and affirmations. Gradually my unconscious stopped sending me negative self-talk and faulty cognitions about myself. As my self-worth improved, it became easier for me to work on desensitizing myself to my fear.

By using your unconscious, you will find that desensitizing is easier than you expected. Go to alpha and relax at least six times a day. Use visualizations and affirmations while at alpha to reprogram your unconscious. In Chapter 15, you will learn how to make an Image Book that will make visualization easier for you. You will be able to see yourself as calm and happy while you are away from your safe place.

The Fourth FEAR-Smasher:
Learning to Risk

Exposing yourself to your feared situation (for agoraphobics that means almost anywhere outside the home) is absolutely essential for recovery. You may feel that it is dangerous to leave your safe place, but there are ways to reduce the anxiety you may feel. Risk asking someone to be your support person, joining a support group, setting goals, and checking off your progress. Your risk will have a big payoff in the form of being able to enjoy activities you never believed were possible for you. Chapter 15 will show you how to make it easy to take the risks of leaving your safe place and also of developing physical fitness as a way of reducing anxiety.

The Fifth FEAR-Smasher:
Sharing Your Gift

We who are agoraphobic have a natural talent for using the fifth FEAR-Smasher. Most of us really are warm and loving people to begin with. We want to help others. However, if we are housebound, or if we are having problems going places and doing things with other people, we may feel we have no practical way to reach out to others like ourselves.

If this is your problem, start small. You can talk to others like yourself over the telephone if nothing else. You can encourage others to try to desensitize. When they try, you can give them "attaboys" and "attagirls," whether they succeed or not. You can point out the positive things about them.

Reach out to the power beyond you to help you desensitize, too. Connie wrote to tell me that she couldn't go very many places without hyperventilating or feeling that she was going to faint. Even so, she had placed an ad in her local paper and asked anyone who had such a problem to call her. One of those who did was a woman who had recovered from agoraphobia eleven years before. She passed on to Connie a prayer that had helped her tremendously: "Dear Lord, please help me to remember that nothing is going to happen to me today that you and I can't handle." Now Connie is using the prayer. It is helping her, and she, in turn, is helping others by passing it on to them. I know other agoraphobics who help each other by writing letters to share experiences and give support.

As you begin to recover, you can take bigger steps. Mike wrote to tell me that with the help of my first book and a phobia clinic, he was overcoming agoraphobia. "But not everybody can afford to go to a phobia clinic. I want to use your book as the basis for a free course that I will teach to anyone who can't afford the phobia clinic. Is that OK?" he asked.

I was delighted. I knew that by reaching out in this way, Mike would maintain his freedom from panic attacks. I also knew how important it had been to me to continue to help others recover from agoraphobia. Now Mike was going to help me reach out to people with whom I would never come in contact on my own.

It's not so hard to share the gift that agoraphobia has brought you. You probably have many ideas about specific things you could do. You need only to get started.

Your Goal Sheet for Getting Over Agoraphobia

Long-Term Goal: On _____ (date) I commit myself to conquer my agoraphobia.

Short-Term Goals:

1. I will keep a journal so that I can know what I am really thinking.
2. I will place blue dots in strategic places and wear a rubber band so that I can confront myself when I am thinking negatively or making "what if" statements (see Chapter 15).
3. I will write down my faulty cognitions and replace them with rational thinking.
4. I will make a list of all my good qualities and affirm my self-worth.

5. I will go to alpha at least three times a day to rest and to reprogram my unconscious.
6. I will make an Image Book (see Chapter 15) to improve my visualizations.
7. I will visualize and affirm myself at alpha as being calm and happy, doing anything I want to do.
8. I will practice desensitizing every day.
9. I will give myself "attaboys" or "attagirls" for working on desensitization, no matter what the results.
10. I will practice rebreathing techniques every day (see Chapter 15).
11. I will give support to at least one other agoraphobic each day.

Agoraphobia: A Gift for You?

Will agoraphobia become a blessing or a bane for you? It can be either. If you take responsibility, set your goal, and use the FEAR-Smashers, it will very likely bring you the gift it brought me. By doing just that, I had my transformation experience and discovered Life Plus. I found that there was a power beyond myself that could help me confront my fear and solve all of life's other problems. It is a wonderful gift that I wouldn't have received any other way.

15

MORE TIPS FOR PUTTING THE FEAR-SMASHER KEYS TO WORK

S o FAR IN PART IV I have shown you how to apply the FEAR-Smasher keys to specific kinds of phobias. Now I want to give you some tips that will be helpful in using the keys for any kind of phobia or fear.

Putting FEAR-Smasher Number One to Work

"*First* take responsibility for understanding your fear and changing your attitude toward it." If you have read this far in this book, you are beginning to take responsibility for your fear. You are learning what it is and what you can do to overcome it. A good way to overcome the temptation to play the victim is to become more assertive. That means taking responsibility for meeting your own needs. It is knowing that it is OK to ask for 100 percent of what you want for yourself, even though you may not always get it.

Dr. Robert Baker, head of psychology at the Ochsner Clinic in New Orleans, believes that if you are agoraphobic, you most likely are failing to act responsibly for yourself. Two areas of neglect, he says, are the inability to recognize, face, and express anger and the failure to take control of one's life.

"Most agoraphobics tend to be very kind, overly nice individuals who are concerned and care for others. But they have difficulty expressing anger. They do not have good defenses against being encroached on by others. They are victimized because they have a difficult time saying no," Dr. Baker said at the Seventh Annual National Conference of the Phobia Society of America.

Agoraphobics aren't the only ones who act this way. If you have any kind of phobia, you may be trying too hard to be nice. You may tell yourself you would be selfish to do things for yourself. You may feel it is up to you to accept the demands of others, no matter how unreasonable they may be or how much you may want to do just the opposite. You may be saying to yourself, "I have to do what others want rather than what I want because I'm not worth the effort it would take to assert myself."

When we give in rather than stand up for ourselves, we are not meeting our own needs. Even though we don't realize it, we may be very angry that our needs are not being met. And then we are apt to feel guilty because of our anger. We start thinking in terms of "my fault" or "fictional fantasies" or any number of other harmful cognitions (see Chapter 6).

Francine wasn't housebound, but she did limit her outside activities because of her panic attacks. Because she was at home so often, her husband and children frequently asked her to do things that they could easily have done themselves. Many times Francine agreed and later felt put upon and resentful. Still, she didn't feel she had the right to be angry. After all, she reasoned, she *was* at home a lot because of *her problems*, so why not help out whenever she could? She would tell herself, "I'm just a bad person because I'm mad."

One day her daughter asked her to type a term paper for her. Francine knew from previous experience that typing the paper meant she would also have to do all the research to write it. This time, however, Francine decided to be more assertive. She looked her daughter in the eye and said, "No, I'm not going to do that. The paper is your homework, not mine." Her daughter couldn't believe that her mother had said no.

"You're going to be at home anyway, and you've got lots of time," she argued.

"But I have other things I prefer to do," Francine replied. Her daughter was angry, but she didn't stay angry for long. Francine felt good because she had been able to assert herself and meet her own needs.

When you are writing in your journal, note the times when you have agreed to do something for someone only because you just couldn't bring yourself to say no. Ask yourself why you couldn't say, "I'm not willing to do that." Then work on affirming your self-worth so that you can say no the next time.

Putting Fear-Smasher Number Two to Work

"Establish your self-worth," says FEAR-Smasher Number Two. Changing what goes on in your head is the best way to do that. Here are some tips for making it happen:

- Improve your ability to restructure your thoughts by polling other people about yourself to see whether you're thinking rationally. When you're in a crowd, do you really look so nervous that others will stare? Ask yourself if others are noticing you or simply going about their business. Ask your friends if you look as if you are creating a scene.

  Jill was a talented violinist who became agoraphobic after the birth of her second son. She became almost housebound and gave up playing in the civic orchestra— an activity that formerly had given her much pleasure. After reading *Anxiety and Panic Attacks*, she began desensitizing herself and managed to go to the supermarket to shop. But she just couldn't bring herself to go back to the orchestra, even though her music was very important to her.

  "I can play the violin at home. My family needs me. Besides, I would have to get a baby-sitter to go to the practice sessions," she told her husband.

Then a psychologist pointed out that she was not being responsible to herself. Her interest in music was a part of herself that she was trying to deny. She was not meeting her own needs. Jill had to admit the real reason she wouldn't go back to the orchestra: She feared that the other musicians might not understand if she had a panic attack and had to leave in the middle of a practice session.

The psychologist suggested that she test whether her cognitions about herself ("Other people won't accept me") were right or wrong.

"Talk to some of your friends in the orchestra and tell them you have had panic attacks. Ask them if they would mind if you had to leave a rehearsal," he suggested. Jill did. The response was overwhelmingly, "We really want you back!" Jill started attending the practice sessions. By using her coping skills, she avoided having any full-fledged panic attacks. She was so encouraged that she began to go many other places, too.

- Be sure to listen to your self-talk and change the negatives to positives. Are you telling yourself, "I can't go to the movies because I might start hyperventilating"? If so, you are programming your unconscious to *make* you nervous at the movies. You are using *fictional fantasies* and telling yourself that because you *feel* nervous, you *are* a nervous person. Affirm instead that you enjoy going to the movies.

Agoraphobia frequently brings on depression, which in turn generates its own negative cognitions. When we have panic attacks, we may be telling ourselves the worst will happen. We think in *white-is-black*, "what if" terms, always predicting the worst possible consequences. To overcome this negative thinking, ask yourself exactly how bad it will be if your worst predictions come true.

If you have a panic attack when you're at a party, just how terrible will it be? Will other people reject you *forever* because you become incapacitated? Very likely the answer is no. If your co-worker seems distant, is it your fault? Instead of playing "My fault!" why not write down all the alternative reasons why the other person might be acting that way. Maybe he isn't feeling well or had a bad day at work. After you have done that, ask him why he is being distant, and you will likely find that one of the alternative reasons was the actual cause of his silence, not anything you did.

- Be vigilant about discovering *when* you are thinking irrationally. Thoughts that put us down are sneaky. We're not always aware that we have them. That is why I used to place blue dot stickers in every room, on the dashboard of my car, and even on my wristwatch. Every time my eyes fell on the blue dot, I asked myself what I was thinking. If I was thinking in negative terms, or if I was feeling bad about myself, I snapped the rubber band I wore on my wrist and immediately countered with a positive affirmation of myself. The blue dots and rubber band helped train me to think in positive terms.

To work on FEAR-Smasher Number Two, write down your cognitions, and counter them with affirmations about yourself. In this way, you will get the most out of FEAR-Smasher Number Three.

Putting FEAR-Smasher Number Three to Work

FEAR-Smasher Number Three's advice to "alpha-program yourself to be free of fear and deserving of self-worth" means using affirmations and visualizations while you are at alpha. In this way, you reprogram your unconscious to become a powerful ally in fighting your fear. The more creative you are with your visualizations, the better.

An excellent way to make your visualizations more effective is to make an Image Book like the ones that members of Agoraphobics in Motion make. Cut out pictures and words from magazines that describe yourself as you want to be. Be extravagant; reach far beyond what you have ever hoped you would be. When you paste pictures of people into your Image Book, do not include faces, so that it will be easier for you to believe the picture is of yourself rather than someone else.

Create a separate page for each aspect of your life that you want to change, develop, or expand. Find pictures that represent yourself looking confident while participating in activities you would like to enjoy. If you want to appear warmer, more loving, or more masculine or feminine, create a page for each of these qualities. Include words and pictures describing you in that way. If you have fears of special places or activities, set up a page that shows you in those situations, being calm, composed, and happy.

When you have made your Image Book, review its pages daily. As you look at the pictures, feel that you are this person *now*. Affirm that you are already as you want to be.

When you go to alpha, use the Image Book to enhance your visualizations and affirmations. Whenever you are tempted to visualize negatively, draw a big red *X* over the scene you conjure up and immediately substitute a picture from your Image Book. In this way you can design more effective visualizations and affirmations. Your unconscious will more quickly become reprogrammed to send you positive cognitions about yourself. Then it will be easier for you to practice desensitization.

Putting FEAR-Smasher Number Four to Work

By using FEAR-Smasher Number Four, you learn to "risk developing your ability to attempt new things." This is important because most phobics feel far too self-conscious to do anything that might cause other people to observe them.

I couldn't help but laugh when I heard what some support groups do to help their members understand that other people rarely even notice what we do in a crowd, much less pass judgment on whether we look nervous or foolish. In one group, members hold a meeting in which everyone is intentionally dressed or groomed in a slightly unconventional manner. Then the others have to try to guess what it is that seems so outrageous. For instance, one woman might polish a single fingernail, leaving the other nails natural. A man might wear mismatched socks. If you have social phobias or agoraphobia, you know how uncomfortable it is to feel that you are dressed inappropriately. You may even feel that everyone is staring at you and talking about how ridiculous you look. But that's just not true. Sometimes people in the support group have to ask each other what they are wearing that is so outrageous. Even though they are trying to identify the social blunder, they can't!

I also know a therapist who leads agoraphobics on exposure trips to a crowded shopping center and lies down on the floor in front of everyone. Strangely enough, people look, but not critically. They do not stop and stare. They simply go about their business.

These are amusing strategies for proving to ourselves that we are not the focus of everyone else's attention. They help us eliminate some of the anxiety we feel about going into the public. They also require us to risk doing something we've never done before. And that is what FEAR-Smasher Number Four is all about—developing our ability to attempt new things.

The most important risk you need to take is to expose yourself to your feared situation. Practicing desensitization is simply acting *as if* you are already free of anxiety and panic. If you find it hard to motivate yourself to do something that has caused you much anxiety in the past, risk trying some of the following tools:

- At home, practice the correct way to breathe in order to control the tendency to hyperventilate when you are desensitizing. Some people who have panic attacks have a greater tendency to hyperventilate under stress than others. When feeling anxious, they breathe rapidly and shallowly in the chest area and bring about an imbalance in the levels of carbon dioxide and oxygen. Hyperventilation causes dizziness, a feeling of nonreality, light-headedness, and sometimes all the other terrifying symptoms of panic. Most doctors advise hyperventilators that breathing into a paper sack for six to eight minutes or holding the breath as long as possible is enough to increase the level of carbon dioxide in their bloodstream and thus correct the imbalance. After doing this, it is easier to take a deep breath.

Dr. Herbert Fensterheim of Cornell University, author of *Stop Running Scared,* told the Phobia Society of America's Seventh Annual Conference that he believes an even better way is to participate in physical activities. He says that if you start to hyperventilate, running in place for ninety seconds or climbing up and down a flight of stairs several times will restore the equilibrium quickly. However, you should not perform these physical activities unless your doctor says you may do so.

You may also want to learn the special *rebreathing* exercises that Dr. Fensterheim believes will prevent hyperventilation. To learn rebreathing techniques, lie on the floor on your back with a heavy book (such as a large telephone directory) on your abdomen. As you breathe, have your support person check to see that only the book is going up and down. Your chest muscles should remain absolutely still. When you are able to breathe in this manner, lower your breathing rate to six to eight breaths per minute. Be sure that you are not sighing or sneaking extra breaths. If the attempts to breathe in this way bring on anxiety, do not abandon your practice. The anxiety will go away as you master this new tool.

After you can breathe properly in a supine position, practice breathing this way while in other positions—lying at a 45-degree angle, then sitting in a slouch, sitting upright, standing, and, as it becomes comfortable, while walking and even eating or talking. By practicing these breathing techniques several times a day, you will train yourself to breathe more normally while you are experiencing stress.

If you do start to hyperventilate while on an exposure trip and because of your panic you cannot force yourself to breathe from the abdomen, Dr. Fensterheim suggests that you try this emergency technique: Pull back your shoulders and arch your upper back in order to make it impossible for you to breathe from the chest. Holding this position for more than a minute may become uncomfortable, but by that time you will probably be able to breathe from the abdomen in a natural fashion.

- With your doctor's approval, begin new fitness routines that will enable you to feel more relaxed while you are desensitizing. Because anxiety is a physical state, you can become calmer if you are healthier. Risk taking up a new sport, provided that your doctor says you may do so. Review your eating habits. Eliminate any substance (caffeine, alcohol, nicotine) that causes your body to increase the symptoms of anxiety.

My new fitness routine was jogging, an entirely new sport that I could enjoy while it brought feelings of calm to my body. I soon found that jogging was helping me reduce my blood pressure and my weight. It increased my self-confidence, too, because when I participated in a meet and made it to the finish line, I could give myself more "attaboys." How terrific I felt! Other fitness routines that helped me to reduce anxiety included eliminating caffeine and alcohol from my diet, reducing my sugar intake, and putting myself on a sensible eating plan that allowed me to lose weight.

- Practice desensitizing as often as you can. Don't give up. Like learning to sculpt, play the tuba, or ride a horse, the skill of desensitizing requires daily practice. If you don't, you won't learn how to do it. Desensitizing is also just like any other skill in that you'll do better on some days than others. I know from experience that on one day you may think you've perfected your golf swing and then the next day hit every hazard on the course. So don't punish yourself if you have been going to shopping malls successfully and then suddenly have a panic attack. Give yourself an "attaboy" or "attagirl" for having practiced, and then go back again the next day. You will master the skill if you keep at it.

- Make use of humor. Not only can laughter help cure disease, as Norman Cousins has proved, but you can also use humor, in the form of *paradoxical intention*, to bypass panic. For instance, when you are standing in the grocery line and feel that light-headed sensation that signals "Warning!" tell yourself, "OK, I'm going to have a panic attack right now, and it's going to be a lulu. I'm going to make it the very worst panic attack anyone ever had. I'll shake so hard everyone will think we're having an earthquake and they'll run screaming from the store. I'll generate so much panic I'll make the smoke detectors go off and the sirens sound and the fire engines come." The more ridiculous the scene you create, the funnier it will seem— and it is likely that your panic will mysteriously dissipate.

Whenever you hear of a new technique that will help your body feel calmer or help you desensitize with greater ease, try it. By taking the risk of attempting something new, you will recover from agoraphobia faster.

Putting FEAR-Smasher Number Five to Work

The exciting FEAR-Smasher is Number Five: "Share the hope by reaching out to help others." Yes, you do have gifts that you can share. If you don't think so, go back to the lists you made about the good things about yourself when you were working FEAR-Smasher Number Two. Did you write that you are a good cook? Then how about baking your favorite dessert and taking it to your elderly neighbor? Did you write that you were a loving person? Risk telling your children, your spouse, your friends that you care about them. Set a goal to reach out to at least one other person every day, even if it only means making a telephone call to encourage someone to practice desensitization.

Expanding the Use of the Keys

The other day I saw a bumper sticker that read, "Leave me alone—I'm having a crisis!" We who have irrational fears are not the only ones who have stress, yet we often tend to blame all our problems on our phobias. Some of the crises we go through may be only the normal life-changing events that everyone has. The wonderful thing about knowing how to use the keys, however, is that we can put them to work to overcome phobias, and we can also use them to reduce the normal, garden-variety kind of stress. Once we have mastered the keys, we can nip life's challenges, disappointments, and hurts in the bud before they flower, go to seed, and sprout up into bramble bushes that can cause us a major crisis.

16

MIND-CHANGING CHEMICALS: CRUTCHES OR WINGS?

P AM WROTE TO TELL ME that she had a "secret" problem: "No one but my husband and mother know that I have such terrible panic attacks that I need a few stiff drinks before I can go to the supermarket, the pharmacy, or the PTA. Drinking never makes me rowdy or silly. It just relaxes me so that I can function normally.

She went on to tell me that her husband had tired of her drinking and had asked for a divorce. Since the separation, Pam's panic attacks had worsened. They occurred even at home, no matter how much she drank.

"My life is the biggest mess I've ever seen," she said. "It's just plain hell, and I don't know what to do about it."

Pam is not the only one who believes that mind-changing chemicals like alchohol, prescription medications, or illegal drugs will lessen the effects of anxiety and panic. Plenty of other nervous people point out that if you have a broken leg, crutches enable you to walk despite your disability. By the same token, they say, if you have panic attacks, why not lean on something like alcohol so that you can keep going, relaxed and free?

The fact is that using the crutch of alcohol is about as helpful as it would be to break a healthy leg in order to help an injured one. The National Council on Alcoholism reports that alcohol ingested over a prolonged period of time may actually *produce* anxiety. The more you drink to protect yourself from panic and anxiety, the more anxious you become. If you drink enough to become addicted to alcohol, you then add bad health and problems with loved ones to the havoc caused by panic attacks. Like Pam, you find that your life turns into a painful mess. You feel helpless to do anything but play the role of the victim.

Any mind-changing chemical with the potential for addiction can lead you down the same painful path. In the beginning, you may feel wonderfully relaxed and calm when you pop that pill, snort that cocaine, or smoke that marijuana. As you continue, however, your body makes a biochemical and physiological adjustment called *tolerance* to the chemical. You have to use more and more to get the same effect. At the same time, you become *psychologically dependent* on it, because you have trained your unconscious to believe that you don't "feel right" without it.

Eventually, no matter how many pills or how much dope or alcohol you take, you don't feel relaxed. In fact, you are now hooked. If you try to do without these substances, you experience withdrawal symptoms—and these symptoms are just as terrible as panic attacks.

Many mental health experts believe that a large percentage of the known 14.7 million alcoholics in the United States have become addicted because of agoraphobia or panic attacks; some also believe that substance abuse can *cause* panic attacks in a person who never had them before. After recovering from the addiction, such a person may experience panic for the first time.

In a recent study on the correlation between alcohol abuse and agoraphobia, Dr. Bruce A. Thyer of the School of Social Work at Florida State University found that 30 percent of the agoraphobics and 33 percent of people with panic disorder in a community-based anxiety disorders support group were alcoholics. Although his research does not indicate whether alcoholism preceded or followed panic attacks, it does show that people who have anxiety disorders are predisposed to alcoholism.

As for prescription drugs like tranquilizers, many people understand that they are addictive, but few realize the havoc they can cause. In her book *I'm Dancing as Fast as I Can*, award-winning television producer Barbara Gordon tells how she became addicted to Valium when it was prescribed for her anxiety attacks. When she tried to withdraw cold turkey (on the advice of a therapist), she had to be hospitalized.

The danger of using drugs recreationally captured the attention of almost everyone in 1986 with the death by cocaine of pro basketball star Len Bias. Those who abused illegal drugs not only had to worry about becoming addicted, but with the public outcry to "do something about drugs," they also faced the anxiety of losing jobs by failing a urine test.

Regardless of whether mind-changing chemicals precede or follow panic, they are bad news. They're insidious, too. Many of us, like Pam, start out using mind-changing chemicals as a crutch that lets us function despite anxiety. We don't realize that in the long run we are adding just one more problem—addiction.

If you feel that you are or have been dependent on mind-changing chemicals, focus on the good news rather than the bad: *There is a way to throw away that crutch and develop wings with which you can fly wherever you want, free and calm.* In fact, because of your experience, you will have insights that others don't have. You can have that if you want it. The first step is to recognize that you are becoming dependent on a substance.

How to Know If You're at Risk

When I started trying to overcome agoraphobia, I was a social drinker. I didn't feel that alcohol was any problem for me, but when I found out that it *increased* anxiety, I cut it out altogether. Not until after I stopped drinking did I realize the advantages of living without alcohol. No longer did I have to worry that I might say or do something while under the influence of alcohol that I wouldn't normally do. I didn't have to worry about lacking the control I needed to drive safely after a few drinks. I could give myself "attaboys" for being a responsible person. All in all, I just felt better about myself.

If you are an anxious person, I recommend that you eliminate alcohol and illegal drugs altogether. If you are taking medication prescribed for your anxiety, find out whether it has the potential for addiction. If it does, be careful. Make every effort to learn the FEAR-Smashing tools that will enable you to cut back the amount you take.

You may not think that any of the substances you are currently using is a problem for you. To learn whether you are in danger of becoming psychologically or physically addicted to any mind-changing chemical, answer the following questions:

1. Do I experience a meaningful change from the use of alcohol or drugs? Do I depend on alcohol or medications to relieve tension, fears, anxieties, or inhibitions?

2. Do I find myself involved increasingly in thoughts about alcohol or drugs? Am I thinking about whether I have enough of these substances when I could be thinking of other things?

3. Do I prefer drinking or taking drugs to associating with family and friends?

4. Do I prefer drinking or using drugs to hobbies I formerly had?

5. Has my drinking and/or use of drugs become more secretive, more guarded?

6. Am I drinking more and more heavily than in the past?

7. Do I ask for medications for pain, anxiety, or sleeping disturbances from more than one doctor, without informing each physician about the other prescriptions? Do I continue drinking even when I know that alcohol

should not be combined with a medication I am taking?

8. Do I tell myself I am handling my problem because I maintain periods of not drinking or using drugs in between binges?

9. Am I kidding myself that by drinking beer or wine instead of Scotch or by smoking marijuana rather than taking cocaine that I am cutting down?

10. When I start drinking alcohol or using drugs, do I end up taking more than I intended?

11. Have I failed to remember what occurred during a period of drinking or using drugs at any time?

12. Do I find it hard to concentrate, pay attention in class, or remember things that happened just a few moments ago?

13. Do I feel guilty, defensive, or angry when someone wants to talk to me about my drinking or use of drugs?

14. Am I sneaking my drinks and/or pills?

15. Have I stopped sipping my drinks and instead find myself gulping or tossing them down quickly? Do I take more of a prescribed drug than the doctor ordered?

16. Do I lie about my drinking or use of drugs?

The answers to these questions will help you decide whether substance abuse has become a problem for you. If it has, I strongly urge you to get professional help. It will be virtually impossible for you to attempt to do any kind of desensitization to stop the panic attacks until after you are free of your addiction. Note, however, that many substance abuse counselors and other community resources may not recognize that panic attacks can *cause* or *follow* addiction. Your panic attacks may be judged as being "only withdrawal symptoms" and ignored. If you have panic attacks and you are addicted, you need help for both problems.

Trading Crutches for Wings

Mary Ann Miller told me that she had her first panic attack at age 12. Years later, when she finally discovered what agoraphobia was, she went through a program that taught her how to desensitize. She improved greatly, but she didn't become free of all her symptoms until she met a minister, Jack Boland, who knew about Alcoholics Anonymous's famous Twelve Steps. He taught her that the same spiritual tools that enable alcoholics to stop drinking could also free her from her anxiety. When she began to think positively and to depend on her Higher Power rather than herself to keep her from feeling anxious, her panic symptoms stopped for good. She was a different person, one who wanted to reach out and help others.

Later Mary Ann founded Agoraphobics in Motion (A.I.M.), a self-help group headquartered in Royal Oak, Michigan. A.I.M. offers a systematic program of recovery through consistent use and practice of ten tools. Nine of the steps are behavioral tools similar to my FEAR-Smashers, such as relaxation, goal setting, visualizing, affirming, and desensitizing. The tenth step includes all of AA's Twelve Steps, reworded to apply to fear rather than alcohol. When agoraphobics incorporate all ten tools into their lifestyle habits, behavioral modification results, leading to recovery.

Because I believe that spiritual awareness is an aid to recovery from irrational fear, I asked Mary Ann how important she felt her tenth step was. Here is what she said:

> We emphasize strongly that each tool is equally important for recovery. The main objective of A.I.M. is overcoming fear through facing the fear by using all the tools. I have found in most cases that behavior modification is generally the prelude to creating or developing a spiritual awareness, which then paves the way for a spiritual renewal or awakening. The quality of the recovery is dependent ultimately on the extent of this spiritual renewal.

Here is how A.I.M.'s tenth step modifies AA's Twelve Steps to apply to fear. The first step reads, "We admitted we were powerless over our *fear* [rather than *alcohol*]—that our lives had become unmanageable."

After admitting that they haven't been able to overcome their fear on their own, A.I.M. members follow AA's other steps to discover their Higher Power and let it do what they cannot do themselves: eliminate fear. They make a commitment to turn their lives over to this Higher Power, which they identify as "God as we understand him." (For many people who have not recognized the spiritual part of themselves, this Higher Power may be the love and support of the group, of one certain person who helps, or even a comforting word or two. They find that they can depend on whatever they recognize as their Higher Power to help free them from panic.) They then take inventory of their shortcomings, admit them to God and to a support person, ask God to remove these defects, and make amends to all whom they have hurt. After they experience a spiritual awakening, they continue to pray, meditate, and reach out to others in order to maintain the freedom from fear that their Higher Power has brought them.

As a result, many people with the dual problem of panic attacks and addiction have recovered from *both* problems in A.I.M. By the time A.I.M. was only four years old, it had five groups that had helped over 500 people.

I discovered the spiritual tools for overcoming fear in a different way. A few years ago, I had a transformation experience that I called Life Plus. It enabled me to know that the spiritual power of the universe was working *in me* to free me from my panic attacks. I found that as long as I did my part, this power could keep me free from fears. My job was to stay in touch with it through meditation, to challenge my negative cognitions, to visualize and affirm myself as being relaxed, and to act *as if* I were calm wherever I went. When I did this, it brought me personal fulfillment on a level that I never dreamed possible.

If, after taking the test in this chapter, you feel that you have a problem with any substance, or even if you feel that you are fully addicted, hold on to the truth that A.I.M. members have discovered. By tapping into the vast resources of your Higher Power, you can become free of fear. You will also have a special sensitivity to others that enables you to reach out in ways that those who haven't overcome substance abuse problems could not. Your crutches will turn into wings as you start living a life of serenity and joy.

Using the FEAR-Smashers to Overcome Addiction

Adele wanted to recover from panic attacks, which she felt had been caused by drugs. During her teens, she had used everything from marijuana to uppers and downers. As an adult, she had even abused heroin for about a year. One day, after a bad experience, she decided drugs had to go. She threw away the needles and stopped all drugs cold turkey. But then the panic attacks began.

"At first I thought I was just having withdrawal symptoms," she wrote to me. "But after two years I was still having them. I lost a good job and my boyfriend because whenever I tried to go anywhere I couldn't breathe. I went to a doctor who prescribed Xanax. Now my fear is controlled to the extent that I can work in a fast-food restaurant, but I'm still not the same person I used to be. I used to hold a *good* job. I used to enjoy dancing, swimming, and being with other people. I can't do those things anymore."

Adele did the right thing in giving up illegal drugs. But she fell into an all-too-familiar trap. She went to a doctor and hid the fact that she had abused illegal drugs. Since he didn't know this, he prescribed a medication that itself was potentially addictive. In effect, Adele threw away one crutch and picked up another. Now she was in danger of becoming addicted to the prescription drug. Moreover, she was depending entirely on the drug to free her from her panic. If Adele wanted a medication, she needed to ask her doctor to prescribe drugs that were not addictive. Then she needed to use the FEAR-Smashers to recover from the panic attacks.

I was much encouraged when Adele told me, "I have come to the conclusion that I caused my panic attacks when I made the decision to abuse drugs. In that case, I believe that I am the one who can also make the decision to take whatever action I must to undo the mess." I felt that Adele had shown that she had determination by her decision to give up heroin. Now she used that determination to take responsibility for her panic attacks. When she began to use the FEAR-Smashers and depend on a spiritual power, she found that with the help of her doctor she could taper off the addictive prescription. Her panic attacks went away, and she was able to find a better job and new friends.

Here are some tips for recovering from panic attacks if you have been a substance abuser:

- Set your goal to attain sobriety first; then set another long-term goal to recover from panic attacks. If you are currently abusing any mind-changing chemical, I urge you to seek professional help. If your problem is severe, you may need to be hospitalized to make it easier and safer for you to recover from substance abuse. If it is not, a group like A.I.M., which offers help in recovering from both substance abuse and panic, may suffice. If you cannot find such a support group, you may need to join a group like AA or go to a private substance abuse counselor first. As you attain sobriety, seek help for your panic.

- Be sure to tell your doctor if you have abused any mind-changing chemical to avoid the danger of being pre-scribed other addictive substances. If you feel ashamed of having to admit to drug abuse or alcoholism, think of the esteem that everyone feels for people like Betty Ford, who have gone public with their battle with drugs and alcohol. Since your doctor sees so many patients who want only to deny that they have a problem with drugs or alcohol, he or she will likely admire you for having the fortitude to try to overcome substance abuse. Remember that your doctor will hold this information in confidence.

- Be aware that the "withdrawal symptoms" you experience may in reality be panic attacks. Even substance abuse counselors and support groups may not know that this is true. If you never had panic attacks before you abused drugs or alcohol but your "withdrawal symptoms" persist for several months, seek a therapist or support group knowledgeable about panic attacks.

- Pay special attention to FEAR-Smasher Number Two—establishing your self-worth. Substance abuse has an insidious way of making you feel guilty and a failure. Watch out especially for *mistaken identity*. Sure, you made a mistake when you depended on a mind-changing chemical to lessen your anxiety. But your mistake is no worse than anyone else's mistakes. With the help of your Higher Power, you can make amends if you have harmed anyone else through your substance abuse, then accept forgiveness for yourself and go on to become the wonderful person you were meant to be.

- Alpha-program yourself to be not just free of substance abuse but also to be a beautiful person with the special serenity that comes from self-acceptance. See yourself developing hobbies, having loving relationships with your family and friends, and doing wonderful things for other people.

- Once you have attained sobriety, risk desensitizing yourself to your fear of panic attacks. Make use of a support person. Plan a weekly practice regimen, and give yourself "attaboys" or "attagirls" for every outing, regardless of results. Remember that you can get over panic attacks, whether they were caused by substance abuse or preceded it.

- Be willing to help others through one-on-one encouragement, involvement in a support group, or even reaching out in ways that have nothing to do with substance abuse or panic attacks. As you bolster your self-worth by reaching out, you will know that you are a wonderful person. You are a part of the marvelous power for good that works throughout the world.

A Thirty-Day Program for Beginning Recovery from Substance Abuse and Panic Attacks

Week Number One:

Day One: Set your long-term goal to recover from both substance abuse and panic attacks. Locate a support group and/or counselor. Plan first to work on the substance abuse.

Day Two: Begin counseling and support-group activity. (*Note:* If you require hospitalization, schedule Day Two immediately after you are released.) If you are under a doctor's care, talk to him about your prescription, tell him or her of your substance abuse, and construct a plan for ridding your life of addictive substances. Tell your family and friends of your intentions.

Day Three: Read AA literature, which will introduce you to the Twelve Steps approach to recovery. Go to alpha and see yourself being helped in your support group. Anytime your mind wanders and you see yourself using an addictive substance, draw a big red *X* on it in your mind.

Continue during the first week at this level.

Week Number Two:

Continue to attend your support group and therapy sessions. Give yourself an "attaboy" or "attagirl" for each session you attend.

Follow the AA approach to finding a Higher Power.

Write ten faulty cognitions about yourself and counter them with positive affirmations. Then create visualizations of yourself as already being the way you affirm that you are, and enjoy these visualizations while you are at alpha.

Week Number Three:
Continue to attend your support group and therapy sessions. Continue to go to alpha six times a day, both for rest and for reprogramming. Affirm that you are a person of worth. Keep a journal, and give yourself "attaboys" or "attagirls" for each day that you maintain sobriety. If your resistance fails and you have a slip-up and use a mind-changing chemical, forgive yourself and start over.

Week Number Four (or after you have been without mind-changing chemicals for at least three weeks):
Ask someone you trust to be your support person to help you desensitize yourself to your panic attacks. Give this person books to read, or have him or her visit your therapist in order to understand your problem. Set up a planned schedule of desensitization to use in the future.

Begin desensitizing, using the same plan as the one for agoraphobia. Continue to affirm your self-worth by reaching out to others who have joined your support group after you did.

17

THE FEAR
OF
SUCCESS

A FEW WEEKS after *Anxiety and Panic Attacks* appeared in the bookstores, my telephone rang. A member of the staff of the nationally televised program *Nightline* was calling.

"We're planning a program on the fear of success," she told me. "Barbra Streisand and Kareem Abdul-Jabbar have agreed to an interview, and we'd like to do a segment on you, too."

I gulped. *The* Barbra Streisand and the man I consider to be the world's greatest basketball player? She wanted to interview *them* on the same show with *me?* I could hardly reply.

"My book hasn't been out long," I stammered.

"Yes, we know. You can offer the viewpoint of someone who has recently attained sudden success."

The opportunity to bring my book to the attention of people who needed to hear what I had to say was too great to pass up. I had to say yes. But as I hung up, I recognized a feeling I'd had before. A small voice inside me was saying, "You're really not so successful that anyone would want to hear *you* on a national TV program. You were just lucky. You don't deserve to be invited to appear on *Nightline.*"

Fortunately, I remembered to use the tools I'd acquired while fighting agoraphobia to silence that insidious voice.

First I set a goal to feel that I was a worthy person who deserved success. Then I took responsibility for restructuring my thoughts.

I sat down and did some rational thinking. Hadn't some of the readers of *Anxiety and Panic Attacks* already written me letters that claimed, "You saved my life!"? If helping others is a criterion of success, this feedback told me I had made it. Didn't I love the little frightened child inside me enough to comfort him and encourage him to go on the program despite his feeling unworthy? Sure, I was OK, no matter what my accomplishments had been, because I was born with self-worth. It didn't matter if my little child felt afraid that others would focus on his bad leg. I, Bob, the adult, knew he was OK despite his fear, and I told him so. I told him I loved him. I began to go to alpha and visualize myself as being a capable, good, worthy person who reached out to others. I pictured myself appearing on TV looking calm and confident.

By the time the *Nightline* van arrived at my door with its crew of three and enough recorders, cables, and lighting equipment to fill a studio, I was no longer feeling unworthy. I had conquered that inner voice, that feeling of dread that I now know was the fear of success. As the crew followed me around during my day's activities, ending up with an autographing party at a Dallas bookstore, I actually found myself enjoying myself and my success.

Celebrities Fear Success, Too

The show was not scheduled to appear until several months later. When at last I did see it, I was amazed to see myself on TV talking about my book and my feelings about success with such apparent calm. I was even more amazed to hear what both Streisand and Abdul-Jabbar were saying. Here were two of the most famous performers in the country telling Ted Koppel that sometimes they didn't feel as if they deserved that success.

I learned a great deal from that program. I discovered that nearly everyone, even the most successful of all, can suffer from the fear of success. I also found that because of the skills I had acquired in overcoming agoraphobia, I was much better off than most people. Maybe I couldn't stop that little child within me from expressing his fear from time to time. But when I heard it, I could reassure him with positive nurturing and rational thinking. I could reach my goals and become more successful than I thought.

Fear of Success: What Is It?

Success, as I define it, is more than possessing a million dollars or being a celebrity. Success is simply being able to achieve happiness in all aspects of your life. It encompasses business, relationships, emotional satisfaction, body image—whatever is important to you.

Fear of success is perceiving yourself as being so unworthy of achieving happiness that you fail to live up to your real potential. You may be very successful in one area of your life, but you still suffer from fear of success if you are not happy in all areas.

You don't feel the fear of success as you feel the physical symptoms of a phobia. Your heart may not race or your breathing become labored. You may have no physical sensations at all. The only thing you may feel is a sense of dread when you are called on to do something unfamiliar to you. It may express itself as a feeling that you are trying to be more successful than your parents or a sibling or a partner and that it's not right to do that. It's feeling that you don't deserve to be happy in everything.

These feelings cause you to limit how much you will risk to achieve success. They cause you to expect to fail, and since expectations are self-fulfilling, you do just that.

If you fear success, you may allow yourself to develop a phobia. A phobia, after all, is avoidance behavior that develops because of irrational fears. In the irrational fear of success, a phobia allows you to avoid the risk of making yourself happy. If you "can't" cross bridges or drive alone, you can't go where others go to have fun, shop for groceries, or visit. You use your phobia to sabotage good relationships with friends and family. Or perhaps you "can't" fly or make speeches. That way, you won't have to do what you must to be more successful in your career.

Fear of success can also cause you to develop migraines, ulcers, arthritis, or colitis. After all, if you're sick, no one could expect you to risk working to make yourself successful.

I can look back and see that the fear of success had me in its grip even in childhood. I was intelligent, but I made only average grades. Why? I didn't see myself as being worthy enough to belong among the good scholars. I studied only to reach the C level that my self-image said was right for me. The first six jobs I had (in the seven years after I received my college degree) told the same story. I would make my sales quotas and be promoted. But once I started receiving recognition for my success, I would sabotage it by going on to a new job, where once again I had to start at the bottom of the career ladder. I did not see myself as being good enough to be in the fast-track group.

When my own business as an executive headhunter began to thrive, I developed agoraphobia and colitis. While stress contributed to the terrible fear symptoms my body experienced, I wonder if I "coped" with my stress by allowing myself to have these physical problems in order to sabotage my growing (and therefore busy and stressful) business!

How We Get That Way

Mental health experts beginning with Freud have equated the fear of success with self-defeating behaviors such as psychosomatic diseases, neurotic symptoms, and substance abuse. They see this fear as developing from childhood situations.

Martha Friedman, of the New York Medical College, explains in her book *Overcoming the Fear of Success* that our self-perceptions determine whether we will fear success. And where do we get our self-perceptions? In her view, our childhood relationships to parents and to siblings tell us who we are. As children, we play the parts that we believe will gain our parents' attention. We may be the problem child, the preferred, the inept, the goody-two-shoes, the dumb, the self-sacrificing, the sick, the smart, the healthy, the precocious, the scapegoat, the court jester, or the runt. When we become adults, we may feel guilty or anxious if we try to rebel against these roles.

Friedman's intriguing book also outlines how we may learn as children to take on guilt we don't deserve. For instance, we may feel responsible if our parents divorced or died, if we had a handicapped sibling, or if we were physically or emotionally abused. The result is low self-esteem. We feel too guilty to be included among the winners in the contest of life. The only way to overcome this fear of success is to get in touch with who and what we genuinely are rather than who and what we perceive ourselves to be. If it turns out that we don't like ourselves as we genuinely are, Friedman writes, we can take responsibility for changing.

Even more fascinating is an explanation given by Dorothy Bloch, a practicing New York psychologist and psychoanalyst. In her book *So the Witch Won't Eat Me*, she theorizes that children often perceive that their parents (who, after all, are only human) are angry or have ambivalent feelings toward them. Because children are small and vulnerable, they may misinterpret their parents' emotions as a wish to kill them. However, since their only defense in life is their parents' love and protection, they cannot allow themselves to think this unbearable thought at a conscious level. Instead, they develop a fantasy that they themselves are so worthless that the parents cannot love them. They work very hard to please the parents (and others) in order to win love. Yet subconsciously they feel that if they overcome the unworthiness, they will not be protected against the parents' desire to kill them. In Bloch's view, this unconscious fantasy persists into adulthood. Unable to think of themselves as worthy, they program themselves to fail whenever success is within reach. She identifies psychoanalysis as the answer to the fear of success.

Is professional help really the only answer? I personally believe it depends on how deeply your feelings of unworthiness are entrenched. Maybe you were an abused child or suffered through some other traumatic events that have wounded you. But maybe you are merely repeating the less than successful role your mother and father demonstrated, simply because their parents provided a similar role model for them. If so, you may be able to use the tools that I did to overcome this barrier to achieving more than you believed possible.

Can the Fear of Success Be Avoided?

I have known lots of people who used phobias to avoid success. Once they saw what they were doing and used my FEAR-Smasher keys, they changed their self-perceptions and eliminated all kinds of fear. When Kay became an unwed mother in her teens, her guilt sabotaged any possibility for emotional happiness from then on. Kay's mother took the child, telling Kay, "You are too young to know how to raise her." Later happily married, Kay longed to have her daughter with her more frequently than the occasional visits the grandmother permitted. But she didn't stand up for her rights because she felt unworthy. She constantly berated herself for having made a terrible mistake. Panic attacks further prevented Kay from being able to take responsibility for her daughter.

"I told myself I was a very bad mother. I didn't feel worthy enough to persuade my mother that I was capable of caring for my own child!" Kay said. To overcome her panic attacks, Kay used my FEAR-Smasher keys. She began to take responsibility for the negative thinking patterns she had developed in childhood. She began to see herself as she really was: a person who made mistakes like everyone else, and a mother whose love for her daughter was great. She wrote down each negative thought about herself and composed a rational affirmation about herself that she could use to blot it out. She reinforced her self-worth by going to alpha and seeing herself as a good and capable mother. Then she took a risk. She *demanded* that her mother give her daughter back. Her mother relented.

Life isn't perfect for Kay, but it is much better than it used to be. She rarely has panic attacks, and her husband and daughter are taking positive steps to learn to live together as a family. Kay also continues to increase her self-esteem by reaching out to help others. She tutors children with learning difficulties, many of whom have poor self-esteem, in a neighborhood school.

"The only reason I couldn't be a reasonably good mother was because I felt so guilty and I didn't believe I deserved to have my own child with me. Once I perceived that I was a good person because I knew how to love, I had enough self-esteem to be able to work on any problems that might come up," Kay said.

No matter how unworthy you feel yourself to be, you don't have to sabotage your efforts to be successful. You can increase your perception of worthiness if you really want to.

How the Fear of Success Can Affect You, and What You Can Do About It

Fear of success can cripple your emotional self, ruin your chances for happiness at work or at home, and destroy relationships with your family or your friends. It can distort the image you have of your body and even cause you to neglect your body. To identify whether the fear of success is limiting you in any of these ways, answer the questions relating to each category on the following list. If it is, study the suggestions for overcoming it.

FEAR OF SUCCESS AND THE EMOTIONAL SELF

1. Do you feel that others can always do things better than you?

2. If something good happens to you, do you hesitate to enjoy it because, "after all, I don't deserve it"?

3. Are the news stories that you talk about the "Wasn't that awful?" ones?

4. Are you always remembering how life treated you badly?

5. Do you find it difficult to spend money on yourself?

If you answered yes to these questions, your lack of self-esteem causes you to see yourself as unworthy and therefore undeserving of success. Perhaps your parents programmed you to become negative because they had to say no to you thousands of times. I believe it is true that few parents say yes nearly enough. When you become an adult, however, it is not appropriate to give those negatives power. Once you are able to love and accept yourself, you can stop putting yourself down and dwelling on your limitations.

Your ability to go after success in any area of your life is limited by poor self-esteem. Here are some simple things you can do to enhance it. Sit down with a sheet of paper divided into two columns. Head one "Liabilities" and the other "Assets." When I did this, I found it was much easier to list liabilities. But come on. What are the good things prople tell you about yourself? Even if you don't believe them, write them down. And what are the good things you know you have done? They don't have to be big things. Just the fact that you are a loving person or one who can understand other people is an asset. Using your talents for cooking, playing tennis, singing, or painting are assets. Your education, knowledge, skills, and interests are assets, too. Every person has hundreds of assets, and I'm only asking you to list ten.

When you write down liabilities, look at them carefully. Then ask yourself if it is really rational to call them liabilities. Beware of generalities, such as Kay's calling herself a "bad mother." Of course she made mistakes. Of course she didn't always know what was exactly right for her child. But neither does anyone else *always* know the perfect solution to child-rearing problems. Because she could offer the most important ingredient of parenting—love—she could not call herself a bad mother.

Now look at your liabilities and set a long-term goal to perceive yourself as a success rather than a failure. Then set up short-term goals that will not seem so formidable to work on. If one of your liabilities is the inability to spend money on yourself, state your long-term goal as "I love myself enough to spend money on myself." Then set up some short-term goals to buy something. (If the pocketbook is flat, you needn't spend a lot. Go to the nearest variety store and buy something frivolous that appeals to you.) Better still, set a short-term goal of rewarding yourself whenever you overcome the temptation to tell someone how life has treated you badly. Overcoming the fear of success works just like desensitization does in getting over phobias. You set a little goal, expose yourself to the actions that are necessary to reach it, accomplish the goal, and move on to another.

FEAR OF SUCCESS AT WORK

1. Would you rather be a follower than a leader?

2. Do you dislike your job but fear making a change?

3. Are you a workaholic?

4. Do you feel you should give in and let others be promoted to the executive level because it wouldn't be right for you to compete with them?

5. Do you feel that you are working at a lower level than the one for which you are really qualified?

If you are afraid to compete, make a change, or be competitive, you carry your fear of success to work. Set goals to enhance your self-esteem.

Psychologists George Dudley and Shannon Goodson in *The Psychology of Call Reluctance* say that 80 percent of persons entering the sales field fail within the first year because of fear of self-promotion. The new salesperson is reluctant to make calls because he thinks that things are bound to go wrong or that he may interrupt or intrude on a prospect. He has a fear of being humiliated or of losing friends if he calls on them. Salespeople who set goals of increasing their perception of worthiness can overcome all these fears. Go to alpha and see yourself as communicating assertively and taking the risks necessary to compete. Use cognitive restructuring both at the alpha level and consciously to increase your perception of worthiness.

It is possible that your fear of success stems from a real barrier. If you yearn to be a psychologist but lack a Ph.D. in that field, the lack of degree is certainly a liability. But it doesn't have to remain one. If it is important enough to you, you can set a goal to get the degree. You can plan the action required to eliminate the liability. Then use alpha programming to see yourself as successful before you take the first step.

If you are a workaholic, set short-term goals to enjoy hobbies, time at home, and activities with friends. You deserve that kind of success, too!

FEAR OF SUCCESS AT HOME

1. Are you a success at work but a failure at home?

2. When something goes wrong at home, do you automatically feel that it's all because of you?

3. Are you dissatisfied with the appearance of your home but "live with it" because it's just too much trouble to change anything?

4. Even when things are going well, do you remind the family of past sadnesses or predict future bad consequences?

5. Do you spend more money than you earn and live by credit cards?

If you answered yes to these questions, you may have a problem with self-esteem, communication skills, assertiveness, and even financial management. Your long-term goal might be "I am happy and successful in my home." Then set short-term goals such as attending assertiveness training classes or going for family or financial counseling. Attending classes in interior design can bolster your confidence to redecorate.

Use self-nurturing techniques to overcome "what if" self-doubts. Jeri wrote me that she hadn't had a panic attack in a long time. She wanted to go back to work and earn enough money to redecorate her house so that she and the whole family could enjoy it. "But I'm scared. I've heard that if you once have panic attacks, you'll always have them. What if I have a panic attack when I am being interviewed for a job?" Jeri needs to tell the little frightened child within herself that she knows she is scared and that she, Jeri, the rational adult, understands, supports, and loves her. Then she needs to go on and start making applications!

FEAR OF SUCCESS IN FAMILY RELATIONSHIPS

1. Do you use sex as a weapon?

2. Do you feel you can't let your spouse and children know when you make a mistake?

3. Do you rely on work and/or outside activities for your emotional satisfaction?

4. Do you feel that if your family knew the real you, they wouldn't love you anymore?

5. Do you often feel dissatisfied with your family and wonder, "Is this all there is?"

If you answered yes to these questions, try to increase your self-esteem and improve your communications skills. Counseling may be in order.

My friend Ardis once told me that she was married to a misogynist. "Mitch hates women. That's why he puts me down." No matter what went wrong in the family, Mitch told her it was her fault. She retaliated by witholding sex, burning the toast, and giving him the silent treatment. She defended herself by trying to appear perfect to Mitch and the children. Not only did she eliminate any possibility for intimacy, but the children reacted to all the family turmoil by getting into trouble. When Ardis made a goal to improve her self-esteem, one of her short-term goals was to become more assertive. She learned how to stand up for herself when Mitch put her down. She decided she was worthy enough to deserve spending money for counseling. Because she changed, Mitch began to change, too. Their improved relationship also had a good effect on the children. Looking back, Ardis says, "I can't believe that I used to be such a doormat. I just didn't see that it was possible for me to act any differently."

FEAR OF SUCCESS IN MAKING AND KEEPING FRIENDS

1. Do you dislike a great many people?

2. Do you feel too shy to let others know that you disagree with what they are saying about politics, your favorite football team, or the weather?

3. Do you always arrive late when meeting a friend, even when you try to be on time?

4. Are you overly generous, aggressive, detached, repelled by people attracted to you, or attracted only to people who are unavailable to you?

5. Do you avoid relationships to eliminate possible rejection?

If you answered yes to these questions, your fear of success takes the form of shyness. While you may have physical, social, and emotional vulnerabilities that make you this way, you don't have to give in to them. Think about the reasons why you believe you are uncomfortable with other people. Is it a fear that others will reject you or think you are not up to par? Do you focus on your handicaps? Are you afraid of intimacy? When you can pinpoint what you are in the habit of thinking, set goals to change it. If, for instance, you always arrive late at parties because you are telling yourself that you know you won't have anything to talk about and everyone will see that you are uncomfortable, you are thinking in *white-is-black* terms. You are so busy predicting failure for yourself that you bring on symptoms of anxiety to which you react by delaying your arrival as long as possible. Write down the truth: You are feeling nervous but you love yourself even so, and *you deserve to have a good time at the party.* Then go to alpha and visualize and affirm that you are feeling calm. (See Chapter 6 for a list of other faulty thinking patterns that may be causing you problems.)

FEAR OF SUCCESS CONCERNING BODY IMAGE

1. When someone tells you that you look great, do you argue that you really don't?

2. When you shop for clothes, do you seek an outfit that will make you look inconspicuous?

3. Do you avoid activities like swimming because you don't want to expose some part of you that you feel is totally unacceptable?

4. Do you find yourself being overly critical of physically attractive people for no particular reason?

5. Do you believe that because of your one secret physical flaw, there's no use trying to attract members of the opposite sex?

If you answered yes to these questions, you are afraid that your body image doesn't measure up to the ideal. And you are not alone. Joanne Wallace, founder of the Image of Loveliness self-improvement courses that have taught thousands of "just average women" to bloom into self-confident, poised people, believes that almost all of us have at least one part of our body that we consider a liability. It could be a too-large nose, crooked teeth, or too much hair or not enough of it. Her "recipe" for beauty is ⅔ cup loving personality, ¼ cup proper posture and positive body language, and 1½ tablespoons good grooming and pleasing appearance. When her students learn to accept the part of their body that they don't like and focus on reaching out to others with love, they begin to feel much better about their body image. Then they learn how to dress to make the most of what they are.

I used to focus so much on my withered leg that I not only felt bad about my body image; I felt that others were focusing on it, too. Not until agoraphobia forced me to focus on my good points did my anxiety about my leg decrease. If you don't like your body image, write down what you don't like about yourself. Go to alpha and use visualizations and affirmations to reprogram yourself to love your body. Then set some short-term goals to learn better ways to dress.

FEAR OF SUCCESS IN CARING FOR YOUR BODY

1. Do you feel you're just a nervous person and therefore there's nothing you can do about headaches, backaches, and stomach problems but take your medicine?

2. Do you feel that there are so many ways to diet that you might as well give up and not use any of them to lose your superfluous pounds?

3. Would you rather fit in with the crowd you associate with (even though they drink too much) than find new companions?

4. Do you feel that because of your limitations, there is no way you can increase your physical fitness?

5. Do you feel guilty if you take time for rest and recreation?

If you answered yes to these questions, you have the fear of success in caring for your body. Rather than go for that great feeling that good health brings, you give up. You may feel that you are just not worth the effort.

After Madge had three babies, her body turned to fat. Then

one day her 5-year-old repeated to her what he had heard the neighbor say about her appearance. It wasn't flattering, and Madge was hurt. Then she decided to use FEAR-Smasher Number One. She took responsibility for her body and made a series of goals to improve. She visited her doctor and set up a weight control diet to follow. Next she set a goal of learning to dress well. She got a color analysis, began wardrobe planning, and learned to use makeup. Each goal was a small step, but as she worked on it, her appearance improved markedly. She *felt* better about herself, too. Because she felt she deserved success, she was able to risk more social involvement and job improvement.

You can use the FEAR-Smashers in the same way to overcome psychosomatic illnesses without depending on drugs or to recover from substance abuse. First, take responsibility for the care of your body. Then establish your self-worth through alpha programming so that you will feel that you value yourself enough to exercise for fitness, eat nutritional foods, and/or get support for your substance abuse problem. When you feel good about yourself, you will know that you deserve to take time for the rest and recreation that will make excellent health a possibility.

If You Can't Do It Alone

If you feel that you can't increase your perception of worthiness by using the FEAR-Smashers, by all means seek professional help. A person trained in the behavioral sciences can help you discover the good things about yourself.

I have a friend whom I'll call Dr. X who was having problems managing his staff. His nurse, bookkeeper, and receptionist were all well-trained and qualified to do their work, but their performance was poor. They did nothing but fight, and Dr. X couldn't seem to stop them. His practice suffered accordingly. Then he consulted a psychologist, who helped him to see that discord and fighting had been the way the doctor's parents had met challenges within the family. Dr. X was simply using the same methods in managing his staff. The psychologist helped him devise a new philosophy in both his personal and business affairs. Dr. X learned to give praise to his staff when they performed well and to listen when they had problems rather than simply insist they do things his way. Now the staff works well together, Dr. X's patient load has increased, and he is happier at home as well.

A Tip from 1407

When I attended the "China, 7000 Years of Discovery" arts and crafts exhibit in Dallas, a model of the Imperial Palace in Beijing caught my eye. Built in 1407, this beautiful complex of 9000 rooms covering 250 acres has been admired for centuries. China has always been an earthquake-prone country, but the Imperial Palace still stands. Why? Underneath the graceful uptilted roofs are nests of corbel brackets. Each of the interlocking joints of these brackets absorbs a fraction of the heavy weight of the roof without passing it on to the next. Thus an earthquake will shake the building, but it cannot destroy it.

You, too, may live in a quake-prone atmosphere because of the negative input you received during childhood, but you don't have to let it destroy you. Each tool you have learned to use in this book can absorb and cancel out a portion of your bad self-image, your low perception of worthiness, or your negative thinking. The ground you stand on may shake, but you will not fall. The strengths you have developed will be a thing of beauty to others throughout your lifetime.

18

THE SECRET OF OVERCOMING THE FEAR OF DEATH

WHEN DAWN LEFT HOME to go to college, she had a hard time adjusting. She missed her family, she didn't like her roommate, and she had to study much harder than she had in high school. Then, right before the first big exam, her mother called with bad news. Dawn's grandmother, whom Dawn had always adored, had died suddenly.

Dawn went home for the funeral, but when she returned, she just couldn't seem to concentrate. She failed the exam. Soon afterward, she had her first panic attack. Eventually she had to withdraw from college and return home.

"I kept having nightmares that I was dying," Dawn told me several years later. "It sounds strange, but before my grandmother died, I never really thought about the fact that someday I would die, too. Suddenly that fact became real to me. And I was afraid!"

Dawn isn't the only one who has told me that the death of a loved one occurred shortly before the onset of panic attacks. Grief increases our stress levels. When we start thinking in "what if" terms about our own death, we run the risk of filling our rain barrels to the spillover point.

Most people seem to fear death, whether they are subject to anxiety or not. Dr. Elisabeth Kubler-Ross, whose *On Death and Dying* is a classic description of the way in which Americans look at death, believes that few people are prepared to deal with the idea of their own demise. Today, most people die in hospitals rather than at home, so children rarely observe and come to grips with the dying process. Furthermore, most of us seem to view death as a taboo subject. We don't talk about it with each other. We keep our children from going to funerals and make up stories about what happened. We say, "Grandpa has gone away," instead of "Grandpa has died." If people we know have a terminal illness, we may avoid being with them. If they try to tell us they are dying, we quickly deny it, assuring them up to their last breath that they will get well.

We can be told over and over that death is just an extension of life, that it is not painful in itself, and that most religions promise an afterlife, but we are still frightened. After all, no one can guarantee us that death is going to be good. We just don't know, and since we don't, we sometimes imagine terrible things. Our unconscious, not knowing the difference between a vividly imagined scenario and real experience, causes our body to generate fear sensations whenever we think about death, just as if we were actually dying.

When you have the psychological, biological, and social vulnerabilities for anxiety, your fear of death may be stronger than the average person's. If being housebound restricts your contacts with other people, or if you are depressed and feel that life has little to offer, you may think about death a lot. The anxiety generated by thinking about death adds to all your other fears and increases your chances of remaining housebound. You don't have to let the fear of death overcome you, however. In my opinion, you can easily eliminate this fear if you take time to develop the spiritual part of you.

How Life Plus Changed My Ideas About Death

Like Dawn, I believe that a death in my family contributed to the development of my agoraphobia. When my father died, my whole world seemed to fall apart. One stressful year later,

I had my first panic attack. Unlike Dawn, however, I didn't have any conscious fear of my own death. Rather, the awful physical sensations that went along with the feeling that I was going to die during each attack caused me to fear the *process* of dying. I told myself that it was terrifying enough that my heart raced and I felt as if I were going to black out and lose control. How much worse would it feel to die? This fear added to my stress levels. It was one of the reasons why I continued to have panic attacks!

My panic attacks went away when I learned to cope with my stress through using the unconscious, thinking positively and rationally, and desensitizing. Not until I had my Life Plus transformation experience, however, was I completely free of the nagging, anxious thoughts that nibbled so painfully at my self-worth and my self-esteem. When I got in touch with my spiritual self, when I knew that I was a part of a loving God and that I didn't have to be afraid of other people, all my fears went away, including my fear of the dying process. Like everyone else, I still don't know exactly what death will be like. But because of my spiritual transformation, I now have faith that it will be a natural part of my existence. I believe that this is the way that you can get over your fear of death, too.

Analyzing Your Fear of Death

Not everyone has the same fears about death. I feared the dying process. Dawn feared the knowledge that she could die. Some people fear that after they die, they will be punished for their shortcomings. Others just fear the unknown.

The first step in eliminating the fear of death is to discover exactly what it is about death that you fear. To discover the basis for any fear that you have of death, assess whether the following statements are true or false:

1. I am afraid because I don't know what it will be like after I die.

2. I am afraid because I will no longer be the self that I am

now, yet I will be no better able to cope with new experiences than I am now.

3. I am afraid because death means the end of all that I am.

4. I am afraid that the process of dying will be painful.

5. I fear death because I will be completely on my own, without the support of my loved ones.

6. I am afraid because I have done many things in my life that are unforgivable, and I believe that I will be punished for them in the afterlife.

Your answers should give you an idea of exactly what it is that you fear. Accepting the fact that you have this fear is an important step. Just as in combating panic, once you accept the fact that you are afraid, the fear begins to lose its grip. You can take responsibility for overcoming the habit of the fear of death by admitting that you are afraid and then resolving to get rid of it by enlisting the help of your spiritual self.

Dealing with the Specifics of Your Fear

If you are worried about not being able to cope on your own after death, it may help you to concentrate on the fact that death is, after all, a natural experience. All forms of life have their natural life span. Nature provides for you to fit in with this cycle just as it does for the rest of all creation. If you are still concerned, remember that you can learn to cope with fears and that you are proving it through using the FEAR-Smashers. You can change from being a fearful person who "can't" do things on your own to a person who knows how to manage fear.

Ultimately, however, I believe that a spiritual approach helps us confront the fears of separation and loneliness better than anything, so I urge anyone who is afraid of death for any reason to seek a spiritual solution.

All religions show us a spiritual way to deal with the fear of death, so if you are already a follower of a religious discipline, you may have either positive or negative feelings about death. If your faith teaches that there is judgment followed by heaven or hell after death and you fear that you will be punished for your sins, you can overcome this fear of death by doing what your religion advises. Sit down and write out the things that you are ashamed of, confess them to God or to a spiritual counselor, and ask for forgiveness. Make amends to those whom you have harmed, and then accept the forgiveness that your faith teaches is possible. Through prayer and meditation, you can experience this forgiveness for yourself.

Other religions teach that you will experience love after death in a much more beautiful way than you ever experienced it on earth. If you say that you subscribe to this teaching but you are still afraid, it is because your unconscious, influenced by the emotion of fear, won't let you believe that the teachings are true *for you*. That's why I want to differentiate between being religious—knowing *about* a lot of religious teachings on love and morals—and being spiritual, which I define as *experiencing* the love and goodness of the power that created you. When you are spiritual, you know with your heart and mind that you have nothing to fear.

I'm not saying that your church, synagogue, or religious community is not a good place to learn how to be spiritual. They can be very good places to promote the search for a spiritual self. Take advantage of all their books, counselors, and the knowledge and support of people in those groups whom you judge by their actions to be spiritual.

Ultimately, however, you become spiritual through an inner search for God, made by you alone. It is a matter of opening your heart up and then asking for and receiving the beautiful experience of knowing you are loved by the creator of our entire universe.

If you are not a follower of religion, another option might be to read books about near-death experiences. Many people who have been technically dead for a few moments before being revived report experiences with great similarities.

Completely free of pain, many feel themselves being drawn through a dark tunnel. At the end of the tunnel is either a heavenly being or a warm, beautiful light radiating love. Sometimes loved ones who have preceded them in death are there to greet them, too. Some people report that the heavenly being or light reviews their life with them, pointing out ways in which they have loved and ways in which they have failed to love. Rather than sensing that the heavenly being will punish them, they are filled with a desire to live their lives differently, more attuned to the love that is being expressed to them. For some persons, the experience is so beautiful that they wish to stay where they are. But the desire to start over and live in tune with their revelation causes them to elect to return to life on earth. Most people who have had such an experience do not talk freely about it, because they realize that all of us who haven't had it would find it hard to believe. Yet the changes that they make in their lives reveal that they have had a profound spiritual experience.

Whether these people actually died or not or saw a true vision of an afterlife, I am not prepared to say. Their experiences, however, can serve to encourage anyone who fears that the process of dying is painful. Regardless of whether these people have really sampled death or not, they have had powerful spiritual experiences that have changed their lives. It is almost impossible to read of these experiences and not want to pursue a search for your own spiritual growth.

How to Become More Spiritual

My Life Plus experience was not one that I planned. In my efforts to overcome agoraphobia, I spent a lot of time at alpha, visualizing and affirming. This process was similar to meditating, although at the time I didn't realize that that was what I was doing. I also read many books on positive thinking that mentioned spiritual pathways. I listened to tapes of people who had discovered their spiritual selves. One day, after listening to such a tape, I had a wonderful feeling of peace I had never experienced before. I was OK, not because of anything I had done, but because God allowed me to love myself. I was now connected to the creator of the universe, and I wanted to love everybody. I was no longer afraid, not even of death.

You, too, can set a goal to become more spiritual and then follow certain steps that will enable you to have such an experience. Here are some ways you can use the FEAR-Smasher keys in your search:

- Be willing to risk. Go to a library or bookstore and look through the many books written about the spiritual life. Read the ones that appeal to you, even if you don't rationally agree with them.

- Set goals to learn how to meditate and pray. If this does not come naturally to you, seek a spiritual counselor or talk to others in your religious community. Set aside a quiet time first thing in the morning to read spiritual literature and meditate.

- Go to alpha and reprogram yourself to become spiritual. If attitudes or actions stand in the way of your becoming more spiritual, visualize and affirm that you are just the way you want to be. Spend time resting in your secret place, letting peace and beauty come into your life.

- Reach out to others. As spiritual giants of our generation like Mother Theresa can attest, spirituality goes hand in hand with loving and helping other people. You can start doing this *before* you feel spiritual, and it will help you *become* spiritual.

- Develop faith. When you just can't seem to stop being afraid, hand it over to God, even when you're not quite sure who or what God is. Like A.I.M. members, you can "put God in your back pocket" and let him take over the fear while you go on and expose yourself to your feared situation. When you try doing this and see that God really does take over for you, you will develop faith.

The Real Benefit of Overcoming the Fear of Death

Dr. Robert Baker of the Ochsner Clinic in New Orleans believes that phobics fear dying *but that they fear living fully even more.* "The object of life is growth and development, and if you don't do that, you get reactions—in the form of panic," he said at the Phobia Society of America's national conference.

Clearly the answer to the fear of death is to stop limiting ourselves and start growing in our relationships, our commitments to others, and our willingness to take chances. If we are totally involved with life, if we are caught up in developing the talents and gifts that our creator has given us, if we are fired by the desire to make a contribution to the world, we will be able to say "so what if" to all the "what if" statements we try to tell ourselves about death.

Former vice-president Hubert Humphrey, riddled with cancer, continued appearing on television and in the Senate until shortly before he died. Busy trying to support legislation that had been his life's work, he had little time to think about death. By living life to the fullest, even under the worst of circumstances, he went on growing and developing to the end.

Yul Brynner kept performing in *The King and I* for months after he knew that his lung cancer was terminal. Wanting to save others from the fate he faced, he made a dramatic and forceful tape to be televised after his death. "When you see this, I will be dead," the tape began, and went on with his urgent plea not to smoke. Brynner was too busy using his talents to help others to let fear of death limit his life.

Maudie, a 77-year-old with the same kind of attitude, wrote to tell me that she had recently developed panic attacks but that she wasn't ready to sit at home, petrified with the thought that she would die. "I have several relatives who are still living in their nineties, so I believe I have many good years left to enjoy my oil painting. I've won several ribbons

and I want to enter some more shows," she said. What spirit!
The FEAR-Smashers and her interest in developing her talents, even at the age of 77, protect her from any fear of dying.

Lisa, a much younger letter-writer, told me that before she
started using the FEAR-Smashers, she had sat at home for
twelve years taking medication and feeling depressed. Now
she is able to work. She also spends her spare time helping
others with panic attacks by giving speeches about her experience. "Two years ago I would never have believed this would
be possible for me," she said.

Your Goal Sheet for Overcoming the Fear of Death

Long-Term Goal: On _____ (date) I commit myself to
overcome my fear of death by increasing my spiritual
awareness.

Short-Term Goals:

1. I will think about and write in my journal why I am
   afraid of death and counter each faulty cognition with
   the truths as taught by my religion or by philosophies
   that appeal to me.

2. I will read books that will help me increase my spiritual awareness.

3. I will spend at least fifteen minutes in the morning and
   fifteen minutes before going to bed meditating and
   praying.

4. I will visualize and affirm while I am at alpha that I
   enjoy meditating, praying, and reading spiritual
   books.

5. When I am in a feared situation, I will hand over my
   fear to my Higher Power.

6. I will develop at least one new hobby so that I can
   spend time enjoying living rather than fearing death.

7. I will reach out to help others as a way of developing my spiritual self.

Is it really possible to get rid of the fear of death? The examples of people who have found courage by continuing to grow and develop to the end tell us that it is. Use the first FEAR-Smasher and start taking responsibility for your spiritual development. You will find that you are beginning a wonderful adventure that will lead to Life Plus.

19

BEYOND LIFE PLUS

I F YOU HAVE FOUND Life Plus for yourself by working the
FEAR-Smasher keys, you are no doubt feeling wonderful. You are completely free of fear, and you can love
yourself and other people. You find the world a very exciting
place to live.

If this has happened to you, I congratulate you. But I want
to warn you that as wonderful as Life Plus is, it's no moun-
taintop on which you can rest and gaze down at the confusion
below. There's still another mountain beyond this one that
you need to climb.

I can explain what I mean best by describing what happened to me. When I wanted to get over my agoraphobia, I set
many goals on which I worked to improve myself mentally,
physically, and spiritually. I overcame the tyranny of a negative unconscious by going to alpha and reprogramming myself with positive statements about myself. I caught myself
when I was thinking negatively, replaced inappropriate cognitions with rational truths, and snapped the rubber band I
wore on my wrist to reinforce new positive thoughts. I acted
as if I were already the way I wanted to be—free from panic
and anxiety. Using these tools, I desensitized myself to all my
fears.

As a bonus, the colitis and diarrhea that had plagued me
while I was an anxious person disappeared. When I saw how

the Five Basic Principles could be used to overcome physical disabilities, I decided I wanted to improve my health in other ways, too. I set goals to lose weight and reduce my high blood pressure and my cholesterol and triglyceride levels. I acted on those goals by following a sensible eating plan, running regularly, and taking time for meditation. I gave up alcohol, fatty foods, and caffeine. The result was that I lost 27 pounds and my blood pressure and cholesterol and triglyceride levels dropped to normal. I felt better than ever.

I set spiritual goals, too. I read books by spiritual authors whom I admired, listened to tapes by positive thinkers, and spent time at alpha, enjoying the feelings of peace and goodness that swept over me. Then I had my Life Plus experience. Suddenly, with little warning, I had a feeling of absolute euphoria! I felt as if I really loved myself and everyone else, too. No matter what mistakes I made, no matter how poorly anyone else treated me, I would never, ever be the old, impatient, angry, frustrated, negative Bob again—of that I was sure.

And my life did turn around. I was completely freed of panic. I loved myself and everyone else. My business improved. My wife and I took a wonderful trip to Europe. Then I felt confident to risk doing something I really wanted to do: change careers and become a public speaker who would tell the world how to banish anxiety and fear forever.

That was what Life Plus did for me. If you have had this kind of enlightenment, you know that it transforms your fear into calm, your negative self-thoughts into positive affirmations, your dreary existence into the joyful fulfillment of using your unique gifts to help others.

If you haven't yet found Life Plus, even after changing habits as I have advocated in this book, you may be wondering why. I believe that a Life Plus transformation can best be achieved when there is a spiritual power helping you to implement the FEAR-Smasher keys. Fear comes from not feeling that you are one with the creator. Without this spiritual wholeness, you can only feel separate and incomplete! The truth is that we human beings are limited in our ability to make ourselves feel secure, forgiven, and happy. But we can tap into a spiritual power that will go beyond what we can do and allow us to feel complete, safe, and fulfilled. I'm convinced that you can have this new way to live if you will set your goal to find it and then use the FEAR-Smashers to attain it.

Now I want to emphasize one more thing. Despite the fact that Life Plus is the most wonderful experience you will ever have, it isn't necessarily a self-sustaining condition. You can receive enlightenment, but if you slide back into your old undisciplined way of living, your fears will come creeping back. To *maintain* Life Plus, you need discipline. Without it, you will regress. Maybe you won't have the phobias and anxieties you used to have, but you won't be living to the fullest, either.

For almost three years my Life Plus experience brought me much happiness and fulfillment. I thought that because I had had this enlightenment, my life would always continue to be wonderful. I didn't realize that I was holding on to this kind of wholeness by carefully monitoring my thinking, watching my diet, and keeping in touch with the spiritual part of me through praying and meditating.

Then, when suddenly confronted by the failure of my marriage and my eventual divorce, I stopped following the routine that enabled me to continue to experience Life Plus. I quit eating healthfully. I started having a few drinks each evening and at parties. I stopped running. I quit meditating. I didn't even go to alpha very often.

I am not knocking myself. When life brings sudden dramatic changes, they can be temporarily overwhelming and can make us feel depressed. Divorce is a tough time for anyone. Like many people, I just didn't have the desire to continue with my usual routine. I'm glad that despite my despair, I didn't fall apart completely. I didn't lapse into panic attacks, even though I could feel my stress level climbing. The reason I didn't was that I still maintained part of the discipline I needed. I used some of the Basic Principles. Whenever I felt the temptation to downgrade myself because of the divorce, I restructured my cognitions. I told myself that I was not unworthy, nor was Cindy. She couldn't help the way she felt, nor was it my fault that she felt that way. I affirmed that we were both still lovable and worthy. I went to alpha and saw us both that way. I continued to visualize myself as remaining calm.

The result was that Cindy and I maintained a very close and friendly relationship despite the divorce, so I avoided the hostility that often goes with the end of marriage. Once the divorce was final, I began to do some self-evaluation and set some new goals for my life. I went to alpha and visualized myself developing a loving relationship with someone new. I then went out and began dating and making new friends. I felt good about the way I was coping with the stresses of being single again.

Once again circumstances intervened, this time in a positive way. *Anxiety and Panic Attacks* became a big success. My speaking career took off, and I began to appear on national TV shows like Phil Donahue's. A feeling of euphoria carried me past the gloomy thoughts I might have had. But still, I didn't fully return to my Life Plus routine of positive thinking, eating right, exercising, and being spiritual.

Then I met Jane. She was beautiful, positive, and charming, and she seemed attracted to me. She was just what I needed— someone to love me, care for me, and make everything wonderful for me again. For about three months I was as exhilarated as if I had sprouted wings and was flying through the clouds. Eventually, however, I began to feel that our relationship was based primarily on physical and emotional needs and that a spiritual connection was lacking. We started having problems, and one day I heard a voice inside me screaming, "This just isn't right. This isn't what you want. This isn't satisfying you."

I told Jane I wanted to keep our friendship but break the relationship we had developed. The discussion that I'd hoped would be rational turned stormy, and we didn't have an amicable parting. Ironically, we were often in contact, because we were both active in the North Texas Professional Speakers Association. Even worse, everyone in the association knew of our breakup. I felt as though everyone were watching us at meetings, at which I felt extremely awkward with Jane.

I tried to tell myself not to worry. By breaking off the unsatisfactory relationship, I was now free to find one that would work. My life would go on. By this time, however, I was 15 to 20 pounds overweight. I ate what I wanted, I seldom ran, and I began watching a lot of TV. The holidays arrived, and I was alone. I wasn't feeling good about my life.

I could feel my stress level rising. I knew I didn't want to relapse into panic attacks, so I was careful to continue to affirm myself and monitor my cognitions so that I could think positively. But something was wrong. What had happened to the joy of my Life Plus experience? I found myself becoming more depressed every day.

On the night of the North Texas Speakers Association Christmas party, I saw Jane across the room and went over to her. But when I reached out to touch her, she shrugged me off and turned away without speaking. I felt that everyone was looking, and I was embarrassed, frustrated, and hurt. The joyous mood of the party was ruined for me. When I returned home that evening, I was in a terrible mood. What was wrong with me? How had I ended up alone during the holidays? Why couldn't I have a friendship with Jane? I didn't sleep the entire night.

This terrible gloom continued throughout the holidays. As I tossed sleeplessly on my bed one night, I made a decision. This mess I was in was bigger than I was. I couldn't handle it alone. I decided I needed to enlist the help of my spiritual self. I began reading spiritual books. In *The Way of the Peaceful Warrior*, Dan Millman pinpointed my problem exactly. He stated that enlightenment, like my Life Plus transformation, is only the *first* step on the spiritual path. To stay on the path, you must follow the *daily* discipline of chopping wood and carrying water—all the tedious, necessary chores—to keep the fires of your spiritual enlightenment burning brightly.

When I read that, the truth hit me in a flash. "You've got yourself far off the Life Plus path," I told myself. "You're not eating or exercising right. You're not praying and meditating every day. No wonder you've lost touch with your spiritual self. And no wonder you didn't feel a spiritual connection with Jane."

I started praying again. I read more spiritual books and went to church. I started exercising, stopped drinking, and changed my diet. Almost immediately I felt better, but still Jane was a burden on my heart. She was the only person in the world that I couldn't go up to and hug and feel positive energy being returned to me.

Another Speakers Association meeting came around. Again I tried without success to speak to Jane. This time, however, because I had been nourishing my spiritual self, I decided that when I went home, I would pray for Jane. That night I spent hours sending her thoughts of love and prayers of healing. I turned this broken relationship over to God and asked him to handle it his way.

At midnight, the telephone rang. It was Jane. "You may wonder why I'm calling you," she began hesitantly, then went on to say that she couldn't stand not speaking anymore. No matter what I felt, she still loved me and wanted to connect with me, even if it was just as a friend.

What an amazing answer to prayer! I then shared with her what I had learned about falling off the path and reconnecting with my spiritual self. We had a very healing conversation and promised ourselves we would get together after she returned from a scheduled business trip.

When we did, we talked for hours. Both of us now realized that somehow we had not taken care of our former relationship very well. Because we had left God out of it, it had been self-destructive for both of us. But now, we both wanted to heal the wounds. We agreed that we wanted to be in each other's lives in some way, even if it was just as friends. We decided to start over, dating as friends, without holding each other to an exclusive relationship. At the same time, we both wanted to work on rebuilding our spiritual selves. We didn't know what the future would hold, but we did know that no matter what happened, we would remain friends. As we practiced our mental, physical, and spiritual disciplines, we knew we could get back on the right path. We would be living the Life Plus way again.

By following the physical and mental disciplines, I got back to my normal weight, and I began to feel wonderful! I was back in the Life Plus mode.

Within a few short weeks, a true miracle occurred. Our relationship had become so wonderful that Jane and I decided to marry.

I now know that if we are to continue to enjoy Life Plus, we must follow a daily discipline so that we can stay connected to ourselves mentally, physically, and *especially* spiritually! We are both committed to doing all the things we must to keep us attuned to our spiritual selves.

From Fear to the Glow of Life Plus

Life Plus is like a violin for Itzhak Perlman to play or a voice for Placido Domingo to sing with. After lifelong practice these artists have attained such heights of musical beauty that our hearts soar whenever we hear them. But both of these artists would be the first to admit that without rigorous exercises and daily practice, they would lose their power to transport us beyond ourselves.

I am convinced that all of us can move *beyond fear* and reach out to claim our own peace and happiness. We can do this by taking the responsibility for changing ourselves, setting new goals, restructuring our faulty cognitions, risking and desensitizing ourselves, and then reaching out to others.

We can be like the common sand and water that through a mysterious process that we don't understand are transformed into precious opals. We may not think of ourselves as perfect. In fact, we may even think of ourselves as being flawed in comparison to others. Yet our differences, like the irregularities of the layers of water and sand in the raw opals, are the very ones that can create a kind of beauty that is distinctively ours. All we have to do is grind and polish ourselves, then expose ourselves to the light that is all around us. Each of our imperfections will then absorb the light and reflect it into the world as a rainbow of colors—a rainbow that glows like no one else's.

That is what Life Plus is all about. It is the mysterious power that transforms you from a fearful person to a being of great value. It will bring you light, beauty, and joy.

Life Plus is worth striving to attain. Once you have it, it is also worth doing whatever you must to keep it.

It is my wish for you that you, too, will find Life Plus and that once you have it, you will keep it forever.

WHERE TO GET HELP AND MORE INFORMATION

Agoraphobics in Motion, 605 West 11 Mile Road, Royal Oak, MI 55184

Dr. Richard O. Anderson, Park Nicolett Medical Center, 7900 International Drive, Suite 870, Minneapolis, MN 55420

Dr. William Anixter, Roundhouse Square Psychiatric Center, 1442 Duke Street, Alexandria, VA 22314

Peggy Arndt, 12011 San Vicente Blvd. (#402), Los Angeles, CA 90049

Dr. Robert Baker, Ochsner Clinic, 1514 Jefferson Highway, New Orleans, LA 70121

Emotions Anonymous, P.O. Box 4245, St. Paul, MN 55184

Captain Bill Evans, Phobia Centers of the Southwest, 12860 Hillcrest, Suite 119, Dallas, TX 75230

Dr. Herbert Fensterheim, 151 East 37th Street, New York, NY 10016

Dr. Michael Freedman, Freedman & Associates, Inc., 24300 Chagrin Blvd., Cleveland, OH 44122

Carol Cott Gross, Fly Without Fear, 310 Madison Avenue, New York, NY 10017

National Association of Neuro-Linguistic Programming, 496 La Guardia Place, Suite 137, New York, NY 10012

PANIC, Inc., P.O. Box 8074, Scottsdale, AZ 85252

Phobia Centers of the Southwest, 12860 Hillcrest, Suite 119, Dallas, TX 75230

Phobia Society of America, 133 Rollins Avenue, Suite 4B, Rockville, MD 20852

Self-Help Clearing House, Graduate School and University Center, 33 West 42nd Street, New York, NY 10036

Toastmasters International, 2200 North Grand Avenue, Santa Ana, CA 92711

Bibliography
and
Suggested Reading

Agras, Stewart, M.D. *Panic*. Stanford, Calif.: Stanford Alumni Association, 1985.

Bach, Richard. *Jonathan Livingston Seagull*. New York: Avon, 1973.

Bandler, Richard, M.A., and Grinder, John, Ph.D. *Frogs into Princes*. Moab, Utah: Real People Press, 1979.

Bloch, Dorothy. *So the Witch Won't Eat Me*. Boston: Houghton Mifflin, 1978.

Burns, David D., M.D. *Feeling Good*. New York: New American Library, Inc., Signet Books, 1981.

Buscaglia, Leo. *Loving Each Other*. Thorofare, N.J.: Slack, Inc., 1985.

Crowley, Mary. *You Can Too*. Old Tappan, N.J.: Fleming H. Revell, 1976.

Dudley, George, and Goodson, Shannon. *The Psychology of Call Reluctance*. Dallas: Behavioral Science Research Press, 1986.

DuPont, Robert, M.D. *Phobia*. New York: Brunner/Mazel, 1982.

Fensterheim, Herbert, Ph.D., and Baer, Jean. *Stop Running Scared: Fear Control Training*. New York: Dell, 1978.

Friedman, Martha. *Overcoming the Fear of Success*. New York: Seaview Books, 1980.

Goodwin, Donald W., M.D. *Anxiety.* New York: Oxford University Press, 1986.

Gordon, Barbara. *I'm Dancing as Fast as I Can.* New York: Harper & Row, 1979.

Hill, Napoleon. *Think and Grow Rich.* New York: Fawcett, 1960.

Kent, Fraser. *Nothing to Fear.* Garden City, N.Y.: Doubleday, 1977.

Kubler-Ross, Elisabeth. *On Death and Dying.* New York: Macmillan, 1969.

Levinson, Harold N. *Phobia-Free: A Medical Breakthrough.* New York: Evans, 1986.

Maltz, Maxwell, M.D. *Psychocybernetics.* Englewood Cliffs, N.J.: Prentice-Hall, 1960.

May, Rollo. *The Meaning of Anxiety.* New York: Ronald Press, 1950.

McCullough, Christopher J. Ph.D., and Mann, Robert Woods. *Managing Your Anxiety.* Los Angeles: Jeremy P. Tarcher, Inc., 1985.

Millman, Dan. *The Way of the Peaceful Warrior.* Tiburon, Calif.: H. J. Kramer, Inc., 1984.

Murphy, Michael. *Golf in the Kingdom.* New York: Dell, 1972.

Nouwen, Henri J. M. *The Wounded Healer.* New York: Doubleday, 1979.

Olshan, Neal, M.D., and Wang, Julie. *Everything You Wanted to Know about Phobias but Were Afraid to Ask.* New York: Beaufort Books, Inc., 1981.

Reich, James, M.D. "The Epidemiology of Anxiety, *Journal of Nervous and Mental Disease*, March 1986.

Ross, Jerilyn. *Learning Theory Approaches to Psychiatry*, edited by J. C. Boulougouris. New York: Wiley, 1982.

Thyer, Burce A., and McNeece, C. Aaron. *Alcohol Abuse among Agoraphobics: A Community-based Replication.* Unpublished Florida State University Foundation Research Grant paper, School of Social Work, Florida State University, Tallahassee.

Wallace, Joanne. *The Image of Loveliness.* Old Tappan, N.J.: Fleming H. Revell, 1978.

Wilson. R. Reid, Ph.D. *Don't Panic.* New York: Harper & Row, 1986.

Zane, Manuel D., M.D., and Milt, Harry. *Your Phobia.* Washington, D.C.: American Psychiatric Press, Inc., 1984.

Zimbardo, Philip G. *Shyness.* New York: Jove Publications, Inc., 1978.

INDEX